YOU'RE MAKING A DIFFERENCE

For a minimum of one year, beginning May 20, 2014, Mister Kleen will donate to the Cancer Research Institute 100 percent of the proceeds ($3.53 for each paperback copy, $2.40 for each Kindle copy) of *You Can't Spend Pride* sold on Amazon.com. Your purchase of this book is making a difference by providing funding to one of the most significant organizations in the fight against cancer.

The Cancer Research Institute (CRI) is the world's only nonprofit organization dedicated exclusively to harnessing the immune system's power to conquer *all* cancers.

This important work has led to a promising new class of cancer treatments called cancer immunotherapy. These treatments mobilize, strengthen, and sustain the immune system's natural ability to destroy cancer cells, wherever they are in the body. CRI awards research grants and fellowships to support scientists at leading research universities and clinics around the world.

To accomplish this, CRI relies on generous support from individuals, corporations, and foundations who have a desire to become partners in their effort to conquer cancer through immunology.

Learn more at CancerResearch.org.

YOU CAN'T SPEND PRIDE

YOU CAN'T SPEND PRIDE

The True Story of
a Family Business
Defying the Odds

Ernie Clark Jr.
and Mary Ann Clark
with Mona Kuljurgis

This book is dedicated to my father,
without whom none of this would have been possible.
We miss you, Dad, and we owe you everything.

Ernest Clark Sr., 1942–2009

Produced with the guidance and services of Social Motion
Publishing, the first and only publisher and publishing-services
provider dedicated to cause-related books and social entrepreneurs.
For more information, go to SocialMotionPublishing.com.

Cover design: Adi Bustaman
Interior design and production: Andrew Chapman

ISBN: 978-0-692-22561-5
Second print edition, May 2014
Printed and bound in the United States of America

CONTENTS

INTRODUCTION

WE'RE A CLEANING COMPANY. WE CLEAN UP AFTER other people. Even though we now spend tens of thousands of dollars on one piece of high-tech janitorial equipment and hold some of the highest security clearances available from the United States government, at the end of the day, we are still a cleaning company.

My father started out pushing a mop in the corporate buildings in and around Washington, D.C. He always used to say, "You can't spend pride." He felt that if you are too proud, arrogant, or entitled to do work you think is beneath you, then don't complain when you can't pay your bills.

Excessive pride was a syndrome my father never suffered from.

Ernie Clark Sr. did not make it past the ninth grade, and my mother never attended college. But they took their janitorial service, Mister Kleen, to almost half a million dollars in annual revenue in the 10 years before passing the helm to me. And in the 28 years since then, as a family, we have taken it to eight figures. None of us have degrees, but what we lack in formal education we make up for in ways that are not taught in school.

Mister Kleen was built on five principles, and these principles continue to drive our company today. They not only make up the five sections of this book but, interestingly, seem to coincide well with the events that chronicle our story. They are:

Work Hard

There's an excellent quotation by the 30th President, Calvin Coolidge:

> Nothing in the world can take the place of persistence. Talent will not; nothing is more common than unsuccessful men with talent. Genius will not; unrewarded genius is almost a proverb. Education will not; the world is full of educated failures. Persistence and determination alone are omnipotent.

Working hard is not just the *only* path to most places worth going; dedication and industry are qualities that can overcome almost any obstacle.

Show Up On Time

I graduated high school at the precise moment my parents desperately needed someone to take over the family business. It was extremely fortuitous timing. I was able to step up because I was prepared, because I had worked hard in the business for many years before then. Showing up on time is not just about the consideration accorded to someone by being punctual, though it *is* that. It's also about preparedness, to be ready for an opportunity when it knocks.

Do What You Say

Quite simply, keep your agreements—by virtue of this alone,

you'll stand out in a crowd. Being a woman or man of your word is a sign of great character, but it also sears you into the minds of your clients, colleagues, and staff as someone they can trust. We train and retrain our staff to ensure we *do what we say*, and we seek to make all our relationships true partnerships so that our words and our actions always stay aligned.

Finish What You Start

Keeping true to your word is an imperative, but finishing what you start is often what's required to keep your word. With the economic collapse of 2008, a tax audit that same year, and my father's passing the next, there were many days I felt stuck in the mire. Hundreds of families depended on Mister Kleen at that point, however, including my own. Though it was often like quicksand, I would have to pull myself out and finish what I started.

Say "Please" and "Thank You"

It may seem like just another platitude on common courtesy, but affording respect to all you encounter is neither common nor trite. It's not only a matter of exhibiting this trait, however. You must ingrain appreciation and respect in the succeeding generations—both towards others *and* for the advantages and privileges bestowed upon them by their parents' and grandparents' hard work.

According to the Family Business Institute, only 30 percent of family businesses survive into the second generation, and 12 percent into the third. I certainly could not have imagined I would end up leading Mister Kleen to a multi-million-dollar business with over 400 employees. But more important, far more important, is that this is still a *family business*—one that now spans three generations. We can truly say that we have defied the odds.

There is an old adage: "rags to riches to rags in three generations." The saying endures precisely because it is so typical for family businesses to achieve success in the first, and sometimes second, generation only to have it slip through the hands of the third. With no firsthand experience of the "rags" beginnings of the story, and with privileges often handed to them, the third generation tends to squander the family's resources. Not only that, it's also common for the first generation to create a successful and viable business, as did my parents, that goes downhill at the helm of the second generation. And of course, the negative impacts of nepotism can have far greater consequences when there's more at stake. Many promising family businesses have fallen to pieces because the principals couldn't manage the *family* part of the business. I understand—it's not easy.

You can't spend pride.

It's a concept I'm intimately familiar with, having cleaned up my share of sewage and sludge. And though you *can't* spend pride, you *can* spend industry, diligence, honesty, perseverance, and respect—working hard, showing up on time, doing what you say, finishing what you start, and saying "please" and "thank you." This is the story of our family and the story of Mister Kleen.

Although the company started in the era of bell-bottoms

and the Bicentennial, the story really began 20 years earlier. I wasn't there, of course, so I'll have the co-founder of our family and Mister Kleen—my mother, Mary Ann Clark—start things off by taking us back to a very different, sleepier time in Washington, D.C.'s history.

SECTION 1

WORK HARD

Mary Ann Barr and Ernie Clark in Washington, D.C., circa 1957.

CHAPTER 1

IT TAKES A VILLAGE

As told by Mary Ann Clark

IT WAS SOUTHWEST WASHINGTON, D.C., IN THE 1950S, and it was different then than it is today. To my eyes, it was a warm, family, working-class neighborhood with tree-lined streets and kids playing ball. It was lovely, and we always felt safe.

But not too far from where we lived there were shantytowns, actual alleys with makeshift tents and shacks where people lived and fires blazed. So much so that our city had an Alley Dwelling Authority. But this fact comes in later in the story. For now, I'm about 13 years old, and the reality that people lived in tents and shacks near our house did not impact me. My life happily revolved around my friends and family and Barney Neighborhood House across the street, a community-based activity center that taught and entertained children after school.

Lucky for me that Barney was so close, not only because it was a fun place to be, but because Ernie was usually there— Ernie, the cute boy from school. I'd known him since fifth grade and now, a few years later, had such a crush on him. After school, I'd rush home, do my chores, and then take off to Barney. Those were fun, carefree days.

Junior high came quickly, though, and disrupted my whole routine when Ernie went off to Jefferson and I was sent to St. Dominic's. Some time would pass before we saw each other again—when the Boys' Club had a Halloween party. After that, Ernie showed up every day at St. Dominic's to walk me home.

I was the oldest of three girls and, with both parents working, in charge of the house and my two sisters. I didn't mind cleaning, sometimes cooking, and tending to the house in general. This paid off in other ways. The neighbors would often ask for help with their kids or some other work. Eventually, I had a little "business" going.

In the summer and on weekends, I took in ironing. Not a particularly difficult task, and I'd charge $4.00 or $5.00 per basket, set up an ironing board in my sunny room, turn on the TV or radio, and get to work. Even though one basket could take me half a day because of the pleated skirts and shirt collars of the Catholic school uniforms, I didn't mind so much. I actually kind of enjoyed it. People would walk in and see the freshly pressed clothes on the hangers and ask if I could iron theirs. I developed quite a following that way. I'd take in $15 to $20 per weekend, always setting aside half in a little savings account I'd opened.

This was back in the days before permanent press and before many people even had clothes driers. In fact, we had an old wringer washing machine, the kind you filled with a water hose, washed your clothes, then ran the clothes through the wringer to squeeze out the water. After your clothes were washed, you'd hang them to dry—winter, summer, spring, and fall—and half the year you just hoped they would dry before they froze.

Ordinary tasks absorbed a lot of time back then, and life revolved around very practical matters. You spent your time dusting and cleaning, vacuuming and washing, ironing and cooking—and of course, raising children, especially if you were a woman. There wasn't all this talk of how to "realize your best life." At the same time, it wasn't so bad at all, and I look back on those days happily.

Ernie, however, had a different life. His mom remarried to a man her family did not like at all. In fact, Ernie's mother's parents—where Ernie and his mom had been living—insisted he remain with them when his mom moved in with her new husband. Pop and Nanny, as we called them, truly adored Ernie. His staying under their roof was to his benefit, but in many ways he still had to navigate the world quite a bit on his own. This contributed to his personality in a way that would serve him well, though—he grew to be a highly dedicated, hardworking person. Even at 13, he was doing more than most other boys, earning his spending money by delivering papers and helping out at the boatyard, sanding boats or whatever they needed. He never waivered, and he demonstrated his ability to work long hours in extreme conditions.

School, Work, Buses, and Schedules

Eventually, the conditions and fires in the shantytowns had become too much for the Alley Dwelling Authority to ignore.

Along with other D.C. government agencies, they decided that Southwest was too run down and that 56 percent of the dwelling units were blighted—which was news to me. Nonetheless, they came in with court orders and bulldozers, called it "redevelopment," and kicked us all out. The only thing left standing in the wake was St. Dominic's Church. Most everything else was leveled.

So, we all moved to the neighboring quadrant, Southeast, and I changed schools to Hart Junior High. Ernie tried living with his mother and stepdad during this time because they had moved to Hart's district when they married, which meant we could attend the same school. Though there were some good aspects to his home—Ernie got along well with his three new brothers, who thought he was very cool and loved having him there—his stepdad never accepted him as part of the family. As ninth grade progressed, Ernie drifted out of school for good, moved back in with his grandparents, and started looking for more employment. That was the last of the schoolrooms to see Ernie Clark and the beginning of nearly 30 years of steady, dedicated work. He was 14.

Despite all this, Ernie and I were now going steady—though, I would have to say, mostly over the phone. This was a problem because my father was fairly strict and commanding—and back in the mid '50s, there wasn't a phone extension in every room. There was one phone, usually in the middle of the house, and within earshot of anyone nearby. My dad didn't like us using the phone in the evenings, and this put a significant dent in my time with Ernie since he often worked into the evenings.

Happily, a solution presented itself. My next-door neighbor

was pregnant one summer, so I'd go over there to dust and mop and run a vacuum, just to help out. Other days, I would just stop by and she, her son, my sister, and I would play board games and watch TV. I simply loved hanging out with her, and it was kind of a reprieve from home. But as much as that, she knew how I felt about Ernie and would let me call him from her house.

Inevitably, my time at Hart Junior High had to end, and my parents enrolled me in Burdick Vocational High School, all the way across town in Northwest. Boy, did it take me a long time to get there. My father and I would leave at 6:15 in the morning, he'd drive me halfway, and then the city bus would take me the rest. Then, coming home took an hour and 15 minutes, changing buses several times. But despite the commute, I truly liked Burdick. I took bookkeeping and English, history and shorthand; all gave me a strong foundation for life in the late '50s. Their curriculum may seem quaint and antiquated now, but I used each and every one of those skills throughout my life—especially as Ernie and I later built Mister Kleen.

Boatyards and Brickyards

During this time, Ernie had a job in a boatyard repairing, refinishing, and relocating boats. It wasn't full-time work, so he soon moved on to a construction company, simply but laboriously hauling bricks around the job site.

Back then, you could buy a car for $100, and Ernie very proudly did. A lot of us got around in that old car for a long time. When it rained or got too cold, bricklaying was put on hold, and Ernie would pick me up from Burdick. When I got a job at a stock company after school, Ernie would pick me up around 7:00 pm or 8:00 pm after work. Then we'd often go to get Ernie's grandfather from his security guard job at 9:00 pm, after which he'd take me home.

Ernie often chauffeured around his three brothers and my sisters as well. We all hung out whenever we could. Ernie's brother Ronnie was about the same age as my little sister, Louise, so we'd drive them around. In fact, one Christmas when she was about five years old, Ernie gave her some Little Golden Books. All these decades later, Louise still has them. He meant a lot to all of us, even back then.

And so it was—around my father's restrictions and Ernie's work schedule, around my high school classes and my job downtown, and around Ernie's grandfather's work and our siblings—that we saw each other. It's hard to think of two people so connected so young, but we truly were. We were really good friends, already for seven years at that point. Time was easy with each other. Two years before, one evening on my porch, Ernie had vowed to always take care of me. Though at the time I took it as the sweet way a boy would say such things, he ended up living up to his promise. Before I graduated Burdick, Ernie asked me to marry him.

CHAPTER 2

MARRIED LIFE IN THE 1960S

As told by Mary Ann Clark

AT THE DAWN OF THE DECADE, WE WERE 17 YEARS OLD, AND we were married. It wasn't so unlike other people our age at that time, but it was fairly different than today when you're still considered a minor at 17. The two of us rented a small, furnished apartment two miles from my parents' house; I would make the walk between them often.

Our newlywed years were happy, and both of us worked full time. Ernie worked seven days a week if he could and eight if the construction company had it. As a bricklayer, 40 hours were never guaranteed because of rain and snow. So eventually, he got a job working with my father at a moving and storage company. Hard to imagine, my father and Ernie working side by side, but there they were. And work Ernie did, incredibly long hours. When he got home at night, his feet were raw and swollen from the hours of lifting and carrying and moving.

Married life transformed more than a few things in my life. One was that my father's opinion of Ernie began to change. My dad did *not* like Ernie when we were younger. Ernie wore a black leather jacket and motorcycle boots, even though he hadn't owned or ridden or probably ever even sat on a motorcycle. From my dad's perspective, this boy looked like a hooligan. But that was the style back then, and he wore it well. My father was not a fan and did his very best to keep us apart.

After we were married, though, my father's view of Ernie softened. He could see Ernie's seriousness and devotion to his own life and to mine, watching him clock long hours to keep our household afloat.

Soon, I had a full-time job at the Department of Agriculture, and not long after came two baby girls—first Cindy and then Dianna. Ernie and I now had a family of our own.

The Pamazzo Brothers

When Ernie lost some of his overtime hours at the moving and storage company, he decided to take a full-time position at Giant Food as well as second job swinging a mop at night. Enter into our life the Pamazzo Brothers.

The Pamazzo Brothers developed quite a few of the high-rise office towers in the Washington, D.C. area, as well as some mixed-use buildings. They had more than a few properties to manage and not enough people to manage them—so when one of the brothers saw Ernie reliably and diligently mopping their lobby floors each night, he asked if Ernie would like to work for them as an area manager. In this role, Ernie would be telling other people how, when, and where to mop rather than pushing it around himself—a nice change.

And so it was that, for almost six years from 1966–1972, Ernie managed a number of the Pamazzo's buildings, overseeing maintenance, repairs, and supplies. But that's not all; he fed their dogs, supervised workmen at their homes, and pulled their boats from D.C. to New Jersey. On the boat-pulling days, I'd go along for the drive. For us, it was like a little vacation.

Unfortunately, and without warning, the Pamazzos' operations shut down. Ernie came into work one day and was told to take the day off. He came in the next day and was told his job had been indefinitely placed on hold, with no explanation. A week would go by before we learned that the Pamazzos had gotten into legal trouble—and Ernie's job was gone for good. There he was, unemployed, with no immediate prospects on the horizon—and now a father of three, with Ernie Jr., having been born a few years earlier.

CHAPTER 3

A WOODEN DOOR ACROSS TWO SAWHORSES

As told by Mary Ann Clark

THANKFULLY, ERNIE'S BIND DIDN'T LAST TOO LONG because he met a man named Kevin Slate, who offered him a maintenance job. As Kevin was just starting his company, he couldn't pay well, and Ernie told him up front that he'd need to move on soon. Kevin seemed to sympathize, and when he got a call for a cleaning contract for a small one-story office building, he decided to pass on it and asked Ernie if he would like to take it instead.

Ernie accepted, knowing he had the four of us other Clarks to assist. The contract was for a company called J.W. Bateson Construction. It was a humble start, and it was my home vacuum cleaner that went out the door each night, but it was our very own client.

The kids and I cleaned Bateson five nights a week. I would get home from a full day at the Agriculture Department, change, we'd all eat, then we'd all jump into our station wagon and head out to Bateson. Little Ernie was maybe five or six then, so he got to empty all the trash cans, while Cindy cleaned the kitchen and Dianna cleaned the bathrooms. I would run the vacuum. Between the four of us, the whole thing would take about an hour. Bateson brought an extra $200 a month into the house, and that really meant something in the early 1970s. In addition, every couple of months all five of us would go over on a Sunday to shampoo the carpets, buff the floors, and clean up around the outside of the building. It was work, quite a bit of it, but we were together.

During this time, Ernie got a full-time supervising job at Ship Shape Building Maintenance. The company cleaned and maintained large office buildings, and Ernie ran a large region of the operation. He was responsible for hiring and firing the employees, the quality of work, keeping schedules, and dealing with client contacts. Other managers just left notes for cleaning crews and went home, but Ernie always stayed to personally do a final walk-through in the evenings—so he had long days.

This is how it went for several years: me at the Department of Agriculture all day, cleaning Bateson with the kids in the evening, and Ernie not getting home until late. During this time, I think Ernie realized that at Ship Shape, the buck stopped with him. He had all of the responsibility, but none of the ownership. After some time, I believe he just thought: *I can do this. I can run these crews, deal with these building managers, negotiate with these vendors, handle these clients, and keep up with all the accounting. I can do this.*

And that was the end of the Ship Shape job and the beginning of Mister Kleen.

Mister Kleen Is Born

The first order of business, we figured, was to come up with a name—and we went around about it for a few weeks. Ernie initially wanted to call it ATEK Maintenance, thinking that being in the "A" section of the phone book was an advantage. I didn't necessarily think so, and when Ernie's brother Ronnie suggested Mister Kleen, we went with it. We decided on "Kleen" so as to not be confused with the cleaning product with the bald muscleman on the label.

With the company name settled, we promptly had stationery printed. I went to our local credit union and, based on my income at the Agriculture Department, got a signature loan for $2,200—not a small sum for an ordinary family in 1976. The payments came out of my paychecks, but with that $2,200, Ernie and I bought vacuum cleaners, mops, buckets, sponges, paper products, soaps, and cleaning agents.

We had a modest but sufficient home in Annandale, Virginia, near the D.C. Beltway, so this would become our office as well. We decided to make the dining room the hub of operations for our new venture. Ernie scrounged up two beaten old sawhorses and placed a scuffed wooden door across them to make our executive desk. We added a phone line, which rang to a rotary phone atop the sawhorse desk, and a filing cabinet was placed in the corner of the room. We had gotten our hands on a vintage 1940s typewriter from my dad. This went onto a rolling cart, which was put in Cindy and Dianna's bedroom—now we had our administrative and accounting department.

In those earliest days, Ernie was determined to build the business by word of mouth—and of course, it wasn't as if we really had money for advertising. But the revenue from Bateson gave us a financial cushion and bought us time for Ernie to get the word out.

Slowly but surely, the business built up. Our next client was a Ford Motor Company facility; coincidentally, their building was not far from Bateson. Every four years around the presidential inauguration, the presidential and vice-presidential limousines would be parked in the Ford garages. The kids and I would mop and sweep up around them. Here we were, scurrying around the giant, tinted-windowed, black, armored limousines that safely whisked President Carter and Vice-President Mondale around. Hard to believe in this day and age that we were allowed near those cars without so much as a background check, but there we were. It's a funny contrast to today's Mister Kleen, when our business has grown exponentially through specializing in high-security client facilities.

Maybe our first few clients did foreshadow the future of Mister Kleen because we also landed contracts with American Security Bank and NS&T Bank locations. It was a point of accomplishment to be trusted with their branches. This was also the time that represented a significant turn for our business. Cindy, Dianna, little Ernie, Jr., and I couldn't clean multiple locations each evening, so this is when Mister Kleen *really* became a family business. We recruited aunts and uncles to help, not to mention the girls' friends… just about anyone we could round up and trust to do the job. It wasn't until about a year or two into the business that we placed our first "help wanted" ad.

Another thing that set Mister Kleen apart was that we always gravitated toward unique and special jobs. This was Ernie's personality. He took great satisfaction in rising to the occasion to overcome difficulty. Probably because he never even started high school, he liked to jump on a project or client that presented an unusual challenge. I think he felt he had something to prove.

Though it was several years later in our history, one particular specialty job comes to mind as a perfect example of what Mister Kleen would take on. Hecht Company, a large department store downtown, needed their hardwood floors refinished. This would seem like a straightforward project, but this location had thousands upon thousands of square feet. Their building was four or five stories high and took up a whole city block. Layers and layers of veneer had built up on those floors over the years, maybe decades. Worse yet, they were open seven days a week, with employee shifts from 7:00 am to 11:00 pm. So, our people would have to do the work during the overnight hours. A daunting task, but we got it done. And we've done many more similarly challenging jobs ever since.

Letting Go of the Day Job

Ernie landed most of our clients through good ol' legwork.

He'd go door to door and building to building to see who needed what done. Mostly, people were happy with their current cleaning service, so Ernie's visits were met with a polite "no, thanks." Even if people weren't entirely satisfied with their service, they were usually not inclined to switch. It's easier to keep the imperfect-but-known than take a chance on something new.

Still, as they say, a "yes" is around every corner, and Ernie's efforts always landed enough yeses to keep the business growing—so much so that in 1981 I could quit my day job at the Agriculture Department. Mister Kleen was now generating enough steam that we no longer needed my regular paycheck. It was a day I'll always remember.

This big shift allowed me to take on Mister Kleen's administrative work. Up to that point, Ernie had been doing most everything—promotion, sales, invoicing, interviewing, hiring, dealing with banks, negotiating with vendors, keeping the books, purchasing, managing our workers, and more. And that's not counting most evenings when he'd check on job sites and even do some cleaning himself. Our daughter Cindy worked in the office part time during a few years, and she was a big help, but most of the administrative tasks had fallen on Ernie's shoulders.

It's a long way into a business before the founder is assured of not having to do frontline work, whatever that may be. Until then, people get sick, they quit, and things go wrong. In the end, it's the owner's reputation on the line.

An Unexpected Turn for the Worse

By the time the mid '80s came along, we'd been in business for nearly a decade. Revenues were pushing close to $400,000 a year, and we had a dozen or so people working for us. The girls were on their own, working for Mister Kleen part time while raising their children. Ernie, Jr., was finishing high school and preparing to be the first among us to go to college. We'd created a successful venture that supported our family, and we were proud of it. Clients all around Northern Virginia and Washington, D.C. relied on us to keep their places looking great—and we did. Despite the inevitable bumps in the road, things had gone well the past eight years. Our hard work had paid off.

But sometimes you don't just get bumps or potholes—sometimes the road drops out from underneath you.

Late in 1984, Ernie, Sr., started getting increasingly intense headaches. This went on for a couple months when, around Christmas, he came down with what we thought was the flu. There wasn't really any reason to connect the headaches to the flu symptoms, but Ernie wasn't one to get sick often, so he went to the doctor. The flu was ruled out, but the physician couldn't determine the cause of Ernie's ailment. He tried a number of different medicines to no avail. One day in February, Ernie went to bed very sick and started talking out of his mind. I called the doctor right away, who said to take Ernie to the emergency room.

The emergency room doctors were also at a loss. What would probably be a few routine imaging tests today, like an MRI or CAT and PET scans, were basically unavailable back then—only a few experimental labs or hospitals, in the entire world, even did them. Eventually, a specialist was called in, who determined that Ernie was suffering from a rare form of meningitis. His brain had swollen from the infection to the point that his very life was at stake. I can't put into words my feelings hearing this news. He was only 42 years old.

At that time, about 60 percent of people who contracted this form of meningitis died, and roughly 30 percent went on to live very impaired lives. Although he never fully recovered and was officially disabled, Ernie became part of the other 10 percent—he'd defied the odds in his life once again.

How could this have happened? What was it that might have so suddenly and mysteriously ended his life? It was pigeon droppings. While doing some exterior cleaning work, he'd been exposed to the dust of dried droppings, which he had unknowingly inhaled. It was a risk almost no one had heard of back then. In 1984, it wasn't common practice for workers to wear protective gear and wet down bird droppings before removing them. It is now.

As immensely grateful as we were for Ernie's survival, it wasn't back to business as usual. While the threat to his life was gone, his health was still very bad. The significant working hours and stress of Mister Kleen needed to end.

We were at a loss. We'd worked our tails off for a decade to build this business. Our entire family income depended on it. There were nearly a dozen other people who counted on us for income. Significant clients relied on us to do our work every day. And then there was all the routine, administrative, paperwork-type stuff to be done. It was a truly difficult time for us, with many major decisions hanging over our heads, all under one encompassing decision—do we keep Mister Kleen going or do we pack it up?

As it turns out, the answer was right among us.

SECTION 2

SHOW UP ON TIME

Ernie Clark Jr.'s senior yearbook photo and Ernie with his parents at his high school graduation in 1986.

CHAPTER 4

PASSING THE TORCH

DAD'S ILLNESS SHOOK OUR FAMILY TO THE CORE. LIFE FELT like an overflowing sink with no way to turn the water off. There was never a doubt that my father would need to take a long, perhaps permanent, break from the business. That he even survived only made it clear he couldn't take any chances. His recovery, to whatever extent possible, was the priority.

This all occurred during my senior year in high school. Though I still worked for Mister Kleen during the summers and on weekends, with classes, homework, and sports, my involvement dwindled. Instead, I was on track to become the first person in our family to go to college. The plan was to earn a business degree, then come back with formal academic training under my belt to help with the company any way I could. It had never been a consideration that I'd run Mister Kleen until the far distant future.

Selling the business was an option for my parents, but the likely sales price would not carry them for very long—especially with unknown medical costs. And there really was not a non-family member who could immediately rise to CEO.

That left us, the three kids.

For my sisters, it wasn't the right timing. Running Mister Kleen would be extremely time consuming, and each had a young child to raise. I was unattached, still living at home, and could devote my full-time focus and attention to the company. So, two options were in front of me: either forego college and take over the business, or go off to college and the business would be sold.

I didn't have to think about it very long. My parents said they would completely understand if I decided to take the school route, but selling the business was unthinkable to me. My sisters, aunts, uncles, Mom, Dad, and I had put in too much effort to just sell Mister Kleen, and my parents very much relied on the income. College would be there. At this pivotal moment, taking the helm of Mister Kleen was probably a once-in-a-lifetime chance.

I had graduated high school. I had worked in the business since almost a toddler. It was a chance for me to take the reins; it was a chance for me to help my parents; it was a chance for me to show up… on time.

CHAPTER 5

LEARNING THE ROPES AND EARNING RESPECT

TO THE BEST OF THEIR ABILITY, MY PARENTS MADE themselves available for guidance and direction, but that wasn't easy. Apart from the mental and emotional load, Dad was fighting back the infection, and my mom was so busy chasing down issues related to his illness—insurance matters, test results, etc.—that she had little or no time for the backlog of administrative work. And of course, there was all the work my dad had been performing every day. These were things I'd largely been sheltered from all this time as a kid, but now they were right in front of me.

My dad was discharged from the hospital and began his slow recuperation at home. As best as he could, my dad gave me a crash course in the ins and outs of Mister Kleen. I spent every moment with him I could, since no one else would be able to teach me what he knew. And of course, I was so immensely grateful that he was still around.

As we worked together, one thing that seared into my mind was my father's lightning-quick ability to estimate a job. It was magic. One afternoon, we went out to bid on a building. The representative walked us around the property, and my father and I asked some questions. Then, sitting in the car in the parking lot, reviewing his notes from our walk-through, I watched him eye the building. He counted how many levels and windows, did some calculations, and *poof...* came up with an estimate—broken down by how many cleaners needed, how many supplies, and how much time. I sat there thinking, *What just happened?* Having only been on the front line of the business, this seemed amazing to me. And it was all done on a yellow pad of paper. That was Dad's system, lots of notes on those yellow pads.

I also learned it was important not to ask too many questions, because he had minimal energy and even less patience. It was soon quite evident he'd be unable to continue working at all. I'd have to jump in the deep end; it would be sink or swim.

"I'm Going to Laugh in Your Face"

Quite frankly, I think there were people at the time who were trying to intimidate me and looking for me to fail. Worse yet, though my parents had hired mostly honest and reliable workers who'd been with them for years, some didn't always merit their trust. Not all parties involved were thrilled to have a barely-out-of-high-school kid in control of their livelihood, and a lot of these guys were at least twice my age. One of them was a long-timer we'll call "Marty."

On a visit to one of our job sites, shortly after taking over,

I opened a supply closet and found Marty—eyes closed, fast asleep. Bad enough if he'd been a worker, but he was a *supervisor*.

Marty was about 50 years old and had worked for my dad for many years. And there I stood, probably younger than his kids. Suddenly, Marty jolted awake. I calmly and quietly told him he was fired. Unhappy about this, he got up from his chair and threw his finger in my face. "Junior," he said, "you're an idiot. And you're going to run this business into the ground." He took one step closer and added, "And when you do, I'm going to come back and laugh in your face."

Still in control of my faculties, I told him, "You're welcome to do that. But as of today, you're fired."

I'm still waiting to hear back from Marty.

"Now Listen Here, Junior..."

But it wasn't just employees who were scrutinizing me. I had to handle the existing clients and vendors as well, some of whom had trouble seeing past my age. For the most part, people learned I had not just fallen into the business the day before, and that I was a chip off the ol' block in many of the right ways. Everyone—except for Bob.

Bob was a client, and he'd worked with my father to the benefit of both of their companies for many years. I was always respectful to him—not just because he was a valued client, but because of his long relationship with my father, and because I believe people should be treated that way. Bob, however, did not share this sentiment. He bellowed orders on the phone, always beginning with his standard opening line, "Junior, Bob here. Now, listen up...."

Junior. That's what they called me. It was to differentiate between my father and me, of course. But the way Bob said it carried a tone, and his treating me like a servant was beginning to rub me the wrong way. One day, he said something that pushed me over the edge, and I told him if he wanted to work with me, he'd have to treat me with respect. Bob condescendingly fired something back, and I told him to go stick it in his ear—or something to that effect.

A few hours later, I got a call from my father. It had been several months into my taking over, and Dad and Mom had moved away to the peace and quiet of the country. Bob called my dad there, after talking someone in our office into giving him the number. My father said Bob had told him about our exchange and my "stick it in your ear" comment.

"Well, what did you say?" I asked.

My dad replied, "I told him you run the company now."

And that was that. My dad's words meant so much to me. It was the end of any lingering doubt over who ran Mister Kleen—and incidentally, the end of Bob as a client.

From Clipboards to Boardrooms

I wish I could say the issue of disrespect was confined to some employees and Bob. These guys—and they were all guys—were in their 40s and 50s. I can understand how young I must've looked. I get it. And some of them felt compelled to keep the youngster in his place. Even in my 20s, the issue still didn't go away.

In 1995, I was in my late 20s and serving as president of our local trade association. At the Touchdown Club in D.C. for a board meeting, this ex-military guy and long-time member stormed into the bathroom and began yelling. He'd gotten mixed up about the start time and was going on in a profanity-ridden tirade that seemed to have little to do with scheduling. Being that he was in his early 50s and likely going through some personal problems, I also wondered if it didn't sit well with him that I was president of the board and young enough to be his son. His finger thrashed in my face as his volume escalated. I calmly finished washing my hands and then turned to him.

"You'd better back the hell up right now," I said. "I don't know who you think you are, but you're way out of line." After I turned to the door, I added, "and that's all I have to say about this matter."

I walked out, went back into the meeting, and acted like it never happened.

It wasn't the only heated encounter I'd have as president. At one point, finances were so bad the group was going to have trouble making it to the end of the year. Meanwhile, a local accounting firm expressed interest in joining—I saw an opportunity in this and struck a deal. I told the firm we'd be happy to have them as members if they'd agree to do the association's accounting. In exchange, we'd waive their membership dues. Those amounted to $250, but their services saved us thousands of dollars per year in accounting fees.

Well, it so happens that the firm they'd replaced belonged to a friend of an association member. At the meeting when we announced the change, this member got loud and red-faced when he heard we'd fired his friend's firm. We all sat there and listened, knowing it was nevertheless the right thing to do.

I've come to realize that good leadership requires taking unpopular stands and upending the status quo—stirring up some hornets' nests I never expected.

Despite the conflict, by the time my term as president ended, that association was back on solid ground, with a sound financial footing and membership that would sustain its mission.

> I've learned many times that lessons often come in packages you don't expect.

Thinking about my experiences then takes me back to my football days. I've learned many times that lessons often come in packages you don't expect. I had a coach in high school who was tough and wielded his clipboard with an iron hand. He demanded respect, discipline, and no excuses. You had to work your butt off twice a day, two to three hours in the morning, and then again in the 90-plus-degree afternoon August sun. Man, I never knew water tasted so good.

Those practices and his guidance toughened me up in ways I could not foresee, for purposes I could not imagine. They solidified a sense of self-discipline, regard, and determination in me that helped translate into millions of dollars in business, and the fortitude to stand my ground when necessary. I am forever grateful for that experience.

Mutual Support

But it wasn't all heated showdowns and power plays. I can honestly say that the guidance and support I've received from my industry's local and international trade organizations are a huge reason for Mister Kleen's success.

Very early one morning, I went to our payroll service to drop off some paperwork and found the door open at Building Service Contractors Association International (BSCAI), which was in the same building. A lone secretary was working early, so I popped my head in to say hello. I'd been meaning to renew our company's membership. I also didn't really know much about the association because I'd never had my nose in that part of our business, and dad had been too busy to attend meetings.

Initially, I absorbed everything I could through the BSCAI magazine, all the amazing information on how to streamline and accelerate your business. That then got me to thinking about the annual convention. I would have loved to go right away, but it was just too big an expense to even consider then. So, two years passed as I diligently socked away money for the trip. When that time finally came, I flew out to the convention and was stunned. I was completely overwhelmed by the support and professionalism of the members—industry veterans from all over the country eager to share their experience and suppliers who taught me to work smarter, not harder. I came home with pages and pages of notes on the many ways we could improve our professionalism, operations, and profit margin.

Our local area industry group, the Capital Association of Building Service Contractors (CABSC), has also been very supportive. And as Mister Kleen has grown, I'm not the only one benefitting from these great groups. Ours are *company* memberships. My niece Christy and nephew Chad are very involved in both organizations; our top management team attends industry events regularly; and my sister Dianna is also a CABSC past president.

"You want to work *for* yourself, but not *by* yourself." That saying is truer than ever, and twenty-five years after popping my head into that open BSCAI office door, we have missed very few conventions and benefit from a long, rewarding, and active membership in BSCAI and CABSC. The camaraderie, community, and education have been invaluable to us.

Education Comes in Many Forms

I have to admit, I've always been a little self-conscious about not having a college degree. In fact, I consider it a crucible of mine. Having a degree feels common these days, and MBAs are around every corner.

But as I'll mention later in the book, this has not been a complete disadvantage. I work twice as hard, always figuring out ways to do things better. I don't feel entitled to my clients—every client is earned, not deserved.

This mindset undoubtedly came from my father. Having left school in the ninth grade, he always pushed his limits, going the extra mile just to prove himself. Not that most anyone would've even known this—but he knew it, and that's what mattered.

On the other hand, I wasn't going to be stubborn about *not* going to college, as if that would be some badge of honor. So, very early in running Mister Kleen, I enrolled in one of the largest and most highly regarded junior colleges in the country—Northern Virginia Community College. What I truly appreciated about NOVA, as it is usually referred to, was that it was made up of people like me, often first in their families to attend college, from middle- or lower-income backgrounds, and as such, who really embraced the classes. NOVA was seen as a privilege and an opportunity, in a way that students at universities sometimes take for granted. Most everyone at NOVA was there because they wanted to be, not because their parents put them up to it. I took as many business courses as I could, determined to fast-track my learning curve and not just rely on the school of hard knocks. Although the classes weren't industry-specific, the instruction was stellar, and I gained so much from my education.

It didn't stop there, however, and never will. Though I haven't taken a class at NOVA in many years, I fully believe in continuous self-improvement—"CSI." To this day, I am always engaged in numerous forms of learning, especially through consultants and coaching. And at any given time over Mister Kleen's history, I've been in two or three groups, always keeping my mind open and sharp. One that I took the initiative to form is Peer Group—a select number of business owners from our industry who share best practices, challenges, and advice on just about every aspect of running our companies. These Peers are in different geographical markets and do not directly compete with each other. This forum began about 14 years ago, and it's one of the best things I've ever done for Mister Kleen.

> A smart man learns from his mistakes— but a wise man learns from the mistakes of others.

So much for the "lone wolf" myth of entrepreneurship.

Because that's exactly what it is: a myth. No entrepreneur is an island, and the most successful among us recognize that everything you know in business you have to learn. You can learn it by yourself, one lesson at a time, or leverage the experience of others. I've always said: A smart man learns from his mistakes—but a *wise* man learns from the mistakes of others.

If I'd been stubborn about doing it solo or was afraid to say, "I don't know," things would not be the same. Life's too short to insist on learning everything alone, one mistake at a time. When you tap into the wisdom of others, you buy yourself more time to make your business great, and more time to make the world a better place.

CHAPTER 6

LESSONS IN CREDIT AND DEBT

CASH FLOW WAS TIGHT WHEN MY PARENTS PASSED MISTER Kleen on to me. Being a small business, we couldn't afford to make a wrong turn. If a couple of jobs just barely broke even—or worse—we could've dug ourselves into a hole quickly.

The biggest chunk of debt was $5,500 we owed a supplier. That may not sound like much today, but it was a lot of money for most people in 1986, including us. Thankfully, Art Veros at Scion Paper had floated us our cleaning supplies for the past few months—but there was a good chance that was going to end soon.

I called him up and asked for a meeting. I explained that my parents had turned the business over to me, and I promised to pay him the $5,500. But I also asked if he could please keep delivering our supplies. Sometimes I wonder what would have happened if Art had made a different decision that day. Life can come down to a handful of crucial moments, and I believe that conversation with Art was one of them. It took some time, but we paid back every penny.

That was my first experience with debt, and I have no tolerance for it. Paying back that $5,500 was slow and painful, and it may as well have been a million dollars. I've remembered that experience to this day. But my attitude toward debt didn't start there. In reality, my dad instilled it in me when I was younger. Having grown up very poor, he had adamant views about money and never wanted to find himself back to having nothing. And in his mind, debt was a road that could lead you back there. Conversely, he was all about savings—as my mom had always been, too. Dad sat me down with my first paycheck and made me put $100 of it into savings. And that was no small portion of my check! Every paycheck I did the same. In his mind, you never buy anything until you have the money for it. It was only due to his medical crisis that Mister Kleen ended up owing anyone anything anyway. But think how bad it would've been if his attitude prior to his illness had been to borrow, borrow, borrow. That unexpected turn could've sunk the company and, in turn, our family finances.

I've kept my father's attitude to this day. Later, when I was almost 30 years old, I sat with some bankers going over company finances, as we were looking to switch banks to better serve our growing company.

"What's your line of credit," they asked, "and how much are you in it for?"

"We don't have a line of credit," I replied.

They looked at each other, puzzled, then back at me.

"Is that a bad thing?" I asked.

"No… it's just fascinating. How did you grow this business to $2 million a year with no debt?"

"We don't buy anything until we can afford it. When we make money and have profits, we invest in new trucks and equipment. Until then, we wait until we do."

It took me two years to save for that first BSCAI convention, and when I did, I paid cash. No credit card company earned interest off that experience.

Sadly, most Americans aren't like this, either in their business or personal lives. Too many live on 110 percent of what they make, aren't very savvy about money, and carelessly take on debt. Not all debt is bad, of course, but few people are good at managing it. The debt ends up managing them.

Even to this day, despite more financial freedom, we operate conservatively. We now have a seven-figure line of credit, but owe zero on it. Nothing. And really, I mainly got it because it was available. You know that joke about how banks only lend you money when you don't need it? Well, that was the situation, and not knowing how the economy would be at some point in the future, it seemed smart to get as a security blanket.

I hear from other CEOs and business people that we're crazy for not leveraging our finances and that our company could be so much bigger. I get that. I know we could. I guess some people can sleep at night with a big load of debt, but I just can't. To me, there's no greater feeling than getting up and getting out of bed, walking through your house, and knowing that you don't owe anybody anything.

CHAPTER 7

THE BUSINESS GROWS UP

THE OLD GUARD THAT HAD BEEN UNDER MY FATHER FOR so long probably thought I was this young punk who'd helped my dad for a few years, then swooped in at first chance to throw my weight around and make radical changes. Well, I'm not sure if it was my intention to throw my weight around, but I did make radical changes.

Image Transformation

The 1970s was a different era, with long hair, beards, mutton-chop sideburns, and smoking everywhere and anywhere. I get that those were different times, but times had to change. First, all workers had to keep their company vehicles immaculate and organized, not smoke in them, and wear their seatbelts. If you smelled like alcohol when you got to work, I'd send you home. Moreover, all cleaning technicians were to be in full company uniform, with shirt tucked and no more than the top button undone by the time they reached the client's property. We were Mister *Kleen*, for God's sake... I couldn't let our employees arrive to work disheveled like junkyard dogs and smelling like ashtrays.

I knew some of the workers were not happy with these changes, but that wouldn't deter me. I wasn't there to win a popularity contest; I was there to get the business back on track. In addition to the new rules on appearance, I also ushered in new systems and procedures. I worked long hours to collect overdue receivables and catch up on our outstanding payables, and I didn't expect anything of anyone I didn't expect from myself. I wanted there to be no doubt that I held everyone, including myself, to the same standards and values.

But regardless of the systems and procedures you lock into place, nothing is ever surefire. And, ultimately, you never know what people are going to do.

One day, I got a call from a client in downtown D.C. regarding the unprofessional behavior of one of our workers. That evening, I got in my car and drove out to the location before the guy's shift ended. I told him his conduct was unacceptable and needed to change. To put it mildly, he didn't handle it well.

He blew up about the situation and started cursing me out, probably thinking his age and size would back me down. But it didn't, and he had clearly taken this too far, so I told him he was fired and needed to leave the property. He ignored that and only got louder, really putting on a show. At this point, he simply needed to be out of the building, and it wasn't my place to drag him out. I called security and, when they arrived, collected his employee badge and uniform. The guards escorted him out as he cursed all of us—the other Mister Kleen workers there, the security guards, me, pretty much the whole world.

But it didn't stop there. Outside the door, he burst out of the guards' hands and onto the plaza.

"This ain't over!" he yelled. "In fact, that's your car over there." He nodded his head toward my car. "I'm gonna break the windows out right now."

I followed him outside, then told the guards to shut the building door and lock it. Now, we're no longer in the building; we're just on a street corner in downtown D.C. And he was no longer my employee.

"We're not on the client's property," I said to the guy, "and you don't work for me anymore. So, if you touch my car, I'm going to kick your ass right here and now."

He walked over to the curb and picked up a big rock. "Go ahead," I told him. "That's all you have to do. I'm not even going to call the police. It's just going to be you and me."

The guard popped his head out the door. "Ernie, don't do that. Don't do that."

I didn't want to, but sometimes you have to draw a line. It wasn't about the car so much—I was thinking about my staff in the lobby watching. This wasn't a macho thing as much as demonstrating to them that I walk my talk. This would be one of those defining moments, when their respect for me as their boss could turn forever. Some of them were pretty much street-raised in rough neighborhoods of the city. This showdown was a language they understood.

We stared at each other for a long moment. Then he put the

rock down, turned, and walked away down the street, cursing me at the top of his lungs the entire block.

In all the business classes I took, they never taught you how to deal with a raging, disgruntled employee winding up to throw a rock through your windshield. People. You just never know what they're going to do. I know people have stuff going on in their lives, and things can get in the way. So, I try to be patient and understanding, but people can mistake this for someone who can't stand up for himself and is easy to manipulate. To which I always think, *Don't let the suit fool you.*

We Are Family

As things got turned around and the company was in better shape, life had shifted around for us as a family too. Far away from conflict-ridden D.C. street corners, my parents were now living in a peaceful and relaxing home in the Northern Neck of Virginia—that peninsula between the Chesapeake Bay and Atlantic Ocean. It was there, over the coming years, that my dad recovered enough to eventually move back to Annandale with my mother, following the birth of my daughter, Lexi. But of course, in the meantime, they were always just a phone call away when I needed advice.

For my sisters, the late 1980s were mostly spent tending to their children, working part time for Mister Kleen, and supplementing the income with other jobs. After I'd been running the company on my own for a bit, Cindy came in full time for a while to help manage the office. But our working together in this capacity wasn't a good match. So we talked it through and decided it would be best for her to work elsewhere. I didn't want the company to succeed at the expense of our relationship, and I didn't want our relationship to succeed at the expense of the company. It seemed the only solution. She agreed, found a job in the insurance industry, and has been working there ever since.

Interestingly, in addition to her part-time hours for Mister Kleen, Dianna had been working for a house-cleaning company, running a couple of crews for the owner. She'd go out with them, make sure the work was done properly, and return the checks to the owner at the end of the day. So, we talked about Dianna working full time at Mister Kleen and starting up a residential division. This was in 1990. The business was on firm ground, and we were well past the transition period between my parents and me. Through the '80s, more and more households comprised two working parents, and as the economy improved, housecleaning became a booming business. We were in a prime position to leverage our experience, operations, and name. It made perfect sense, and Dianna was the perfect person to run it.

Dianna started this division exactly how our dad started Mister Kleen—she went door to door handing out flyers and talking to people about housecleaning. While some companies might have bought a vehicle or two, hired additional employees, and rolled out a promotional campaign, we'd have none of that. Dianna cleaned the initial homes we picked up. Then, after we'd established a need we could fill, we hired someone. A little later, we hired two more people. And so on. Within a couple years, we were running several vehicles a day. Ultimately, the residential division became an integral part of the company, and Dianna led it to total more than a hundred client households at its peak.

My family also grew to include someone else during these difficult but rewarding years—my then girlfriend, Danyelle. She and I had started dating in high school, and throughout this time became closer and closer. In school, I had a regular window-washing job in the summers at a high-rise not far from our office (the headquarters for Mobil Oil where Danyelle worked for 15 years after graduation). I'd work up and down the gleaming glass all morning, and then Danyelle would bring me lunch. We became the best of friends. In the winter, I also cleared snow at client properties, and she'd often ride along in the truck with me, sometimes pitching in to shovel snow herself. She even helped me dig out one time, when the truck got stuck in the snow in the middle of the night.

And I'll never forget when we had to do late-night stakeout duty. One of our longtime clients complained that our crew was continually setting off the alarm system, which is no small problem because it leads to costly fines for the false alarms. Our crew contended they weren't doing anything wrong, but the client insisted otherwise. So Danyelle and I set ourselves up in a car in the dark parking lot, like a couple of undercover detectives, to check up on the crew. Sure enough, they were right—turns out the alarm system had a glitch.

Much in the way my parents met young and really connected, so it was with Danyelle and me. We bonded over the ordinary aspects of life and work, just as my parents had. So, it's not particularly surprising that, a few years later, Danyelle and I got married—and not many years after that, we ended up working together in various capacities at Mister Kleen.

❖ ❖ ❖

As my parents celebrated their 30th wedding anniversary and my dad's partial recovery, a new decade brought a new Mister Kleen. We were now servicing both commercial and residential clients; Dianna was in the family business full time; and solid processes, automation, and systems were in place that greatly improved our operations. During my four years at the helm, from 1986–1990, we'd grown more than threefold—from just under $400,000 in annual revenues to $1.2 million. It wasn't that we could rest on our laurels, but we'd come a long way. We had become, as we would later call ourselves, a family-owned business *and* professionally managed company.

SECTION 3

DO WHAT YOU SAY

Mister Kleen field team shown with company vehicles
in front of the office at the Clark family home in the 1990s.

CHAPTER 8

DISCIPLINE AND CRUCIBLES

NO SMALL TASK, ALMOST TRIPLING REVENUE IN FOUR years. I was happy and grateful. But I had no time to waste. You have to finish what you start, and so would I. True to form—mine, as well as my father's—there would be no leasing of expensive commercial space or extravagant celebrations. To celebrate and invest back in the business, with my parents' agreement, I had an addition built onto the family home in 1990 to serve as extra storage and a conference room for what was now our million-dollar business.

Restraint. My friends called it discipline. It had been ingrained in me since the day my dad sat me down, made me put that $100 from every paycheck into savings, and taught me to read the stock pages. But I don't just say this as a display of bravado or mental toughness. I thank my lucky stars every day those qualities were drilled into me, because the long road to success is not always straight and smooth. In fact, most often, it's winding and rocky.

Mister Kleen is a federal contractor, along with many other companies in the Washington D.C. area. Friends often ask me what that's like. Well, it's like this: the bidding process is gargantuan. Courting a client can take years. Hundreds of hours go into estimating a job and creating the proposal to bid on it. In the end, we're bidding against four or five other companies. You never know how it's going to turn out. It's true that our contracts are for sometimes multiple years at a time. But, here's the kicker: all of them come with a 30-day cancellation policy. Thirty days, that's it. If your client isn't happy with you or your work, you have 30 days to pack up your stuff and go. And that's whether you spent five or ten thousand dollars acquiring the client, whether you invested tens of thousands in new equipment and hiring employees, whether you implemented custom systems and procedures to accommodate their facility, or not. It's still 30 days. So when people ask how long our contracts are for, I simply tell them "30 days at a time."

It's funny, when I first took over the business, I'd meet up with my friends on their holidays or spring breaks from college, and they'd say, "Ernie, why are you busting your butt so hard? What's wrong with you? You're always at work. Come hang out. Come to this party or that." I missed a lot of parties back then, including my first couple class reunions, one of which I couldn't attend because of an emergency clean-up at a downtown hotel after a fire.

I did, however, make it to my 20-year class reunion. It was great to see everyone, but in contrast to what my high school buddies were saying before, I got a lot of, "Hey, Ernie, I heard you're doing really well. Must be nice."

Yeah. Must be nice. Funny how it wasn't so nice when I was cleaning up charred sludge on a Saturday night. The *doing-really-well* fairy must have smiled down on me, the stars aligned, and the luck of the draw was in my favor.

It can be a bit annoying at times. As if whatever success we've attained has nothing to do with the 14- and 16-hour days my family and I worked; nothing to do with shoveling full city blocks of snow at age 13; nothing to do with working hard, showing up on time, doing what we say, finishing what we start, and saying "please" and "thank you."

You Can't Spend Pride

My parents didn't go to college. Neither did my sisters. And I only took some classes, never earning a degree. Perhaps that's why people suggest luck brought us here. Perhaps that's understandable. But my family and I know better. When my father and I worked the business decades ago, we knew we may well be the most uneducated people in the room—so we listened, we took notes, we focused, and we never took anything for granted. In our off hours, we were constantly reading, constantly learning.

There's a pervasive cultural paradigm that says a college degree is your ticket to the good life. The problem with that quasi-myth is that it's only partially true. A college degree opens certain doors down certain paths; that's absolutely true. But once through those doors, everyone has to work hard, often learning from scratch a trade or business they've only come to know in books. I've seen a lot of people go to college, get a degree, and think that they're entitled to a certain level of success because of it. In their defense, it's the bill of goods the colleges sell. But then I've seen their graduates sit around and wonder why they're not successful. They won't work hard because they have a college degree—and they went to college thinking they could avoid hard work—but they sit around and wonder why success hasn't shined on them. It's sort of a tragic irony.

Researcher and statistician Thomas J. Stanley is co-author of *The Millionaire Next Door* and its sequel, *The Millionaire Mind.* In his work, Stanley profiles the characteristics of America's deca-wealthy, those with high individual net worth rather than simply high incomes. In his research, he discovered that a disproportionate number of very wealthy Americans *do not* have college degrees. It's an interesting statistic. And I gather it has something to do with the false expectations heaped upon college students by the ones doing the heaping.

> Never let arrogance and vanity interfere with your goals.

It's a myth that you can't do well in life without a college degree. You absolutely can. You just have to never let arrogance and vanity interfere with your goals. As my father always reminded me: You can't spend pride.

An inflated ego and sense of entitlement—favorite and prolific qualities among some Americans—won't pay the bills at the end of the day. Both my mother and father were keenly aware of this, and made my sisters and I aware of it too. There's not a day that goes by that I'm not grateful for that lesson and, as a result, I always make sure that humility, an open mind, and a willingness to learn are the backbone of Mister Kleen's work.

I Thank God for Lazy People Every Day

Crucibles often drive the course of people's lives. Any test or trial or tough situation that forces you to make a difficult decision can mark your path for the rest of your life. I guess not having attended college is a crucible of mine. But in having to endure that crucible, I have come to an important realization: *I thank God for lazy people every day.* They make my job easier because they make our company look better (as long as they aren't working for us!). Lazy people have trouble with working hard, showing up on time, doing what they say, finishing what they start, and saying "please" and "thank you." And because they do, because that laziness creeps in, our ability to follow these principles only makes us stand out more.

And this brings it all around again to discipline—restraint and discipline in your work life, in your profession, in your finances, and in your relationships. If you can harness it, you're well on your way to achieving your life's aspirations.

CHAPTER 9

TRUE PARTNERSHIPS

WHILE I FIND DISCIPLINE AND HUMILITY TO BE KEY traits of my success in leading Mister Kleen, neither would matter much if our employees did not carry out their work with care and finesse. This is why we seek to create true partnerships with our employees. We expect a lot from our staff, and we push them, but we also treat them with a great deal of value and regard. We know our overall success depends on how we recruit, manage, and motivate our people. Reading and understanding people is imperative because, ultimately, *they* do the job. On account of this, we refer to our staff and vendors as *internal clients,* and foster solid, long-lasting relationships with them. If our *external clients*—our customers—are the reason we're here, then our internal clients are what keep us here.

In addition to rigorous training, we also focus on employee recognition programs, strict safety standards, competitive pay, and comprehensive benefits, and make sure our workers have everything they need to do their jobs properly.

And the beauty of *that* is, when you take care of your

internal clients, they not only take care of you, they take care of your external ones as well.

Newsletters, Leaf Blowers, and the Client's Perspective

I'd love to share with you the many amazing stories of our adept and savvy employees, but I'll limit it to just a few. One I like to tell is about a great guy who worked for us only part time in the evening. He was at his day job, also a cleaning tech position, and listening to the client there berate and bemoan the cleaning company that employed our part-timer. The client was complaining that the staff was not performing, that communication with the management was sloppy, and that he was still waiting to hear back from a phone call he'd placed a week ago. The cleaning tech came back the next day with one of our newsletters, *The Kleen Sweep*. He handed it to the client, saying, "Mister Kleen is the company I work for in the evenings. They're good people. You should be talking to them." They did talk to us, and more than that, they requested a proposal. More than ten years later, they're still our client.

Another incident happened just a short while ago with one of our biggest clients. I only know about it because the client relayed this story to me at a recent lunch. By sheer coincidence, and unknown to any of us, this client's company bought a commercial office building right next to one of our existing contracts. One sunny day, his staff was out in front of this building preparing for a pre-marketing photo shoot, but the entrance was strewn with leaves and debris. So, in suits and skirts and heels, his team was sweeping and crouching to clean the front entrance. As they tell it, all of the sudden, a guy appeared from the next parking lot and asked if they needed any help. Relieved for the offer, they gratefully accepted. The guy went away, then came back moments later with a leaf blower. In less than a minute, he cleared the entrance of all the leaves and debris. The staff had no idea who he was, except that he was wearing a Mister Kleen uniform. Conversely, our cleaning technician had no idea the people he just helped were employees of one of our biggest clients. After our client relayed that story, I told him, "You know, the only thing that could make that story better is if we got the chance to bid on the cleaning contract to that building." He laughed, and agreed.

And the dedication to our work extends up the ranks as well. It's been said around the office many times that Dianna would go to any length for an employee or client. Here is but one example, as told by a client:

> Some years back, when I was managing a three-building, mid-rise commercial center in Tyson's Corner, I needed to swing by my office to pick something up on a Saturday afternoon at about five o'clock. Dianna Clark, the Vice President of Operations, and one of her regional supervisors were literally on their hands and knees inspecting and cleaning the main lobby floor. They had no idea I was going to be stopping by the building, so this was not staged in any way. It speaks volumes of a company when you see management in the trenches.

Steve Nadler (right) celebrates the opening of the new 8,000-square-foot Mister Kleen headquarters in 1999 with Ernie Sr. (left) and Ernie Jr. (center).

We treat our employees well, and they treat us well, because my mother and father laid the foundation for it decades ago. Same goes for vendors. One of our true partners through our history is Steve Nadler. He is our long-time accountant and, over the last 30 years, has become a good friend. In fact, I used to mow his lawn when I was 13 years old. Steve took on my parents' business back in the early 1980s and has been a key player in our evolution ever since. I've always appreciated how he looked out for us. In fact, one snowy winter back in 1986, when the New York Giants played the Denver Broncos in the Super Bowl, I dug Steve's car out of a massive snowdrift just in time for him to catch his plane to California to see the big game. To hear him tell it, that was the day he pledged his undying loyalty to our family. It was a lucky turn for us.

Steve knows a lot about my parents' business in the early years, and he was gracious enough to share some of his knowledge:

"Ernie, Sr., treated people very well—in an industry where people were *not* treated well. He succeeded in a very competitive, cut-throat industry; it was *not* an industry for the weak or the meek."

"If you had a dictionary in front of you and looked up the term 'street smart,' Ernie Sr.'s picture would be in there," says Steve. "He kept his overhead down and worked out of his house. He worked smart but wasn't greedy; he didn't take his first dollar and buy an expensive car. He and your mother had it all—street smarts, native intelligence, and they did everything they could to survive. They wouldn't quit."

Steve Nadler has been such a great resource to all of us over the years. He is a superb accountant, a trusted counselor, and a great friend. Thank you, Steve, for your memories and perspective on my parents' history.

Trust Your Gut

With vendors like Steve, trusted and supportive employees, and streamlined systems, you'd think that things would run smoothly most of the time. And most of the time, they do. But once in a while, despite our best efforts, we go for a partnership that just wasn't meant to be. And oftentimes, these can be lessons in listening to your gut.

A while back, we had a contract with a large federal client to do all their carpet cleaning and flood-restoration work. They were truly huge, with more than one million square feet of headquarters space over three buildings. The facilities-management company that oversaw all the mechanical, engineering, and maintenance of their buildings was also huge, with billions in annual revenue (that's billion, with a *b*). Like us, this company's contract with the federal client was not indefinite. They had to re-win it every few years. Because the facilities-management company knew Mister Kleen's systems, procedures, and past performance, they wanted us in the bid. This was important to them and lacking with their janitorial subcontractor at the time. They also knew our flood restoration work with this client and knew they were happy with us.

So, the facilities-management company sent me the contract specifications. It was structured like a labyrinth, with too many intermediaries and too many hands in the cookie jar. Other factors caused me to hesitate as well, but mostly, it was my gut telling me, *No.* I knew by this time that my gut had become a fine-tuned instrument, and I'd learned to see a bad deal coming down the road—mostly because I'd been through a few. This deal just didn't feel like the right fit for us.

I called my contact and explained that, though we really appreciated the opportunity, we were going to respectfully decline this offer.

Dead silence on the phone. I thought he'd fallen out of his chair.

Once he collected himself, he said, "Ernie, you amaze me. I don't know anyone else who would pass on this opportunity."

We hung up the phone amicably. Still, two weeks later, I got a voicemail pleading with me to reconsider. "You're a great fit… the client loves you… we'll re-win this together."

Hmmmm. It would be big money, but it didn't sit well with me. I was out of town at a conference and decided to let my sister Dianna, who'd become our Director of Operations, make the decision. The management company must have been pretty forceful and persuasive, because upon my return, I learned that we'd signed on to bid. We ultimately won the deal.

It didn't take long for me to realize that my gut had been

right all along. The management company tied one arm behind our back the whole time. They interfered with our ability to run things left, right, and center. It was, without exaggeration, just about the worst two years of my career, despite the fact that the federal client did like us and were, overall, happy with our work.

Nevertheless, two years later, when their option year came up again with our contract, the facilities-management company fired us and rehired the low-bid company they'd had there previously.

Nice. Lots of our time and effort wasted. And I'd had the feeling it was going to happen all along. I appreciated Dianna's willingness to take on the risk and challenge associated with this deal. She and our operations team worked very hard to make this work, but in the end, it wasn't meant to be.

Listen to your gut, especially if it's backed by experience. Those early warning bells almost never steer you wrong.

Listen to your gut, especially if it's backed by experience. Those early warning bells almost never steer you wrong.

CHAPTER 10

MY 60/40 RULE

Relationships and Performance

At the time of this writing, Mister Kleen is in the top 10 percent of our industry in revenue—an achievement that's taken my family 38 years to accomplish. I'm proud of our success, but I'm even more proud of the quality of our work, our relationships with our clients, and our reputation out in the world. As hard as we've worked to put our business on sound financial footing, we have worked even harder to build a solid, steady, high-quality company that will endure the test of time.

Over the years, I've hired a lot of attorneys and consultants for guidance on how to grow and sustain our business. I can't tell you how many times I've heard, "Put the pedal to the metal. Make as much money as you can, fast, and get out" or "Sell, get out, and do the next thing." I've heard some variation of this advice a lot, but I never hired any of the attorneys who gave it.

Truth be told, we could be three times as big as we are today.

My ultimate goal in building Mister Kleen, as it was for my parents, is to create true partnerships, among our clients, our vendors, and even our employees. This may sound like pie-in-the-sky idealism, but you'll see that it has an extremely practical component as well. And if you're going to create something of quality, something of integrity, something that's going to last, it's the only way to go.

Reputation

So, the quick-fix, cut-and-run, cash-out strategy is definitely not for us. And we hope our work and our history demonstrate that. In fact, most of our clients come through referral and word of mouth, and that's on account of our reputation.

I care a great deal about Mister Kleen's reputation and work very hard to sustain a good one. In fact, one of my goals has been to cultivate a positive reputation among our competition. *Your competition?!?,* you may think. Yes, our competition. It may sound like a far-fetched goal, but your competitors certainly have the greatest motivation to talk badly about you. So, if you can get them to say something positive, it's truly an accomplishment. And it's not just an altruistic ideal, nor coming from wearing rose-colored glasses. I can't tell you how many times a potential client who, for whatever reason, couldn't hire the cleaning company of their choice later said to us, "We brought up your name to this or that company, and they were very complimentary about you. They said you were a fine operation, a class act, that you've been around for a long time and are good people."

When I hear feedback like this, it's a defining moment. You can't always control everyone's perspective or words about you and your work. But if you do right by most people most of the time, the truth will bubble up. Your competition doesn't have to praise you—they are, after all, your competition—but we work so hard at what we do that, when I catch wind that someone has said something like this about Mister Kleen, I know our reputation precedes us. And that's what my mother, father, Dianna, and I have aspired to all along.

I'll close on this point with some nice words of support by a recently acquired client. This is what makes it all worthwhile.

> Good Day, Mr. Clark:
>
> I would like to thank you and the whole Mister Kleen Team for all of the time you have spent throughout this janitorial proposal process. You have provided us with a very qualified proposal and detailed interview. Your staff projected passion, confidence, dependability, and accountability. These character traits are some of the foundations of the way XYZ Contracting does business, and how we stand out as a company…
>
> I am happy to inform you that XYZ Contracting has selected Mister Kleen Maintenance Company Inc. to be awarded the new janitorial services contract for the ABC Building.
>
> Congratulations on this new and hopefully very rewarding relationship!

60 Percent Relationship

Your reputation precedes your relationship, and your relationship supersedes your service. Even though we spend a tremendous amount of time improving our performance, in these past decades I've found that your relationship with the client trumps even your performance on the job. It seems like those should be reversed, but they're not. Fully 60 percent of your success with any client relies on your communication, and 40 percent on the quality of your work. This is because, when you are servicing clients and facilities of this magnitude, it's simply expected that you know how to clean! So the issue is, *what more do you bring to the relationship?* Everyone, especially when money has been placed on the table, likes to feel valued, heard, and regarded. It's horrible to feel dissatisfied with something, have a question you're not comfortable asking, or feel like you've been left flapping in the wind. Keeping the lines of communication open, easy, and positive is imperative to maintaining healthy client relationships.

> 60 percent of your success relies on your communication, and 40 percent on the quality of your work.

We feel this is so much so that we actively seek out communication with the client. Built into each one of our contracts are regular performance benchmarks we elicit feedback on, and they all culminate in our scheduled client-partnering meetings. We'll chat about the big game or current events, but we also come in with a highly organized written agenda designed to evaluate our performance over the previous 90 days and discuss the upcoming quarter. In this way, we're able to draw out any issues or problems that need to be addressed and drive home the fact that we aspire to keep the lines of communication open and flowing.

40 Percent Service

But then, it isn't all communication, is it? Forty percent of your success *is* about the quality of your work, and most people would be amazed to know all that goes into it. Cleaning large-scale commercial buildings does *not* look like the cleaning you do at home—in fact, it's nothing like it. Our industry is perceived to be a low-tech, easy-point-of-entry business. However, to do the job right, it's fairly complex and highly technical. A lot of science goes into it.

When we bid a job, we take into account the entire scope of our work over long periods of time. We precisely measure how many square feet of carpeting there is, as well as hard-surfaced flooring. We count the number of bathroom fixtures, conference rooms, break areas, employees, desks, and much more. We estimate the amount of supplies needed for each project and, most importantly, we calculate our production rates. Production rates are the amount of time it takes our cleaning technicians to perform each task properly. Our production rates are broken down in tremendous detail—to the point of, *It should take you this long to clean that bathroom fixture.* We live and die by our production rates; they determine if we make a profit on a job, break even, or lose our shirts.

And the job is not just systems and production rates. The

equipment has changed, too. When my parents started out in 1976, they used a household upright vacuum cleaner, sometimes straight out of my mother's living room. In the late 1980s, we moved to backpack vacuums where the vacuum canister straps to your back. And six years ago, we moved to ride-on vacuums, which look kind of like a Segway, but clean your carpet while they move you around. With each vacuum-cleaner iteration, we've increased our production rate significantly.

Perhaps it's being of my generation versus that of my parents, but I've always felt that investing in technology would help differentiate our business and help us to work smarter, not harder. Around 1990, we purchased our very first computer, before many people I knew had even seen one. My wife and her mom came over for a few evenings and got it all set up for us. The funny thing is, Dad came by soon after that, when he was in town for one of his regular doctor's visits and saw the "fancy" new computer and printer. He looked at me with a rather stern face, looked back at the computer, then back to me, and said, "I sure hope you know what you're doing spending all this money." For a man who'd happily used pencils and legal pads not too many years before (and it served him well), it was quite an adjustment. Not surprisingly, when we ultimately bought our building in 1999 and set up computers in all the offices, as well as copiers on both floors, he just shook his head and said, "I can't even imagine what all this cost."

Those were smart investments, and we've made many more to improve our technical capabilities. We do this not just to stay competitive and satisfy our clients, but also to make the jobs of our employees easier. If you've ever had to work with the wrong tools, you know how frustrating it can be—and the end product of your effort is usually not as good as it should be. As I wrote at the start of Chapter 9, take good care of your internal clients—your employees—and they'll take good care of your external clients.

Green Kleening

Leading our industry, however, is not just about production rates, technology, and client relationships—it's about being at the forefront of transformations in the way our industry plays a part in the world. One example is green cleaning, which has become significant in recent years as people have become more aware of the harm chemicals can do to their health and the environment.

> Take good care of your internal clients—your employees—and they'll take good care of your external clients.

Being among the top 10 percent of our industry, Mister Kleen has the capacity to do more harm or more good. We certainly want to fall to the side of the latter. People spend a huge chunk of their lives at work, often in closed spaces, so we feel it's important that our cleaning methods and products are as safe as possible. For us, green cleaning is a standard, not an option.

Because of this, we are actively building and refining our green cleaning program, which we call, of course, "Green Kleening." We are a member of the U.S. Green Building Council and are actively pursuing a Green Seal GS-42 certification, which establishes healthy environmental requirements for commercial cleaning service providers. As many of our clients are pursuing green initiatives, we are also available for professional guidance on obtaining the highest levels of Leadership in Energy and Environmental Design, LEED, certification—currently the most comprehensive and respected standard in the green building movement.

> You are a steward of all you have and a caretaker of all you touch.

With a responsibility for servicing millions of square feet of commercial space, we know our work can affect the lives of literally thousands of people every day. Furthermore, we all have to live with the affects of cleaning products and processes on our air and water, so it's our duty to ensure we do our part for the better.

❖ ❖ ❖

I've always believed that you are a steward of all you have and a caretaker of all you touch. This means being mindful of all the ways Mister Kleen affects the lives of our employees, their families, our clients and their clients, the workers at our client facilities, and society as a whole. I continue to do my best to see that Mister Kleen gives back in every way it can, so that we leave the world, whenever that may be, a better place than we found it.

SECTION 4

FINISH WHAT YOU START

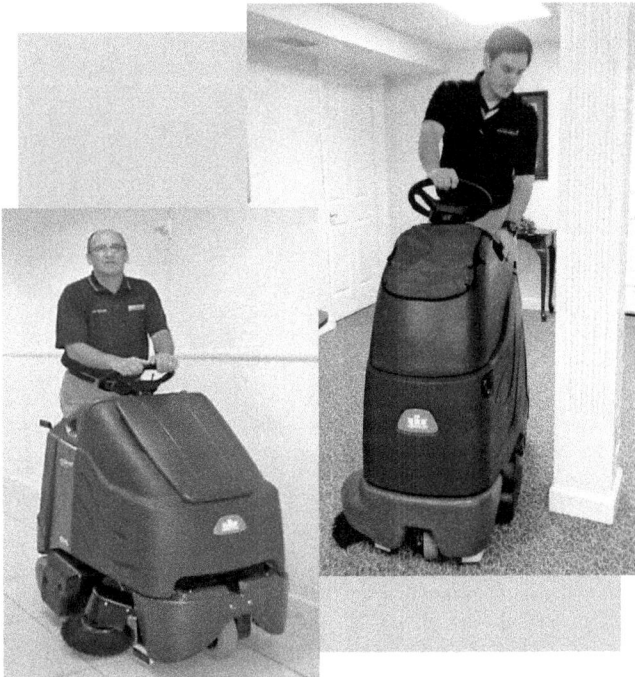

Mister Kleen moved into the 21st century with ride-on vacuum cleaners in multiple sizes to maximize productivity.

CHAPTER 11

A NEW CENTURY BRINGS NEW FOCUS... AND NEW CHALLENGES

AS 2001 ARRIVED, MISTER KLEEN WAS IN VERY GOOD SHAPE.
We had definitively established ourselves within our market, gained the respect of our industry, and now had the third generation of our family involved in the business. We'd grown to annual revenues of a few million dollars and bought an 8,000-square-foot building to headquarter our operations under one roof. I felt like there was some leeway to finally slow down a bit, after the long marathon to get there. Little did I know a huge change was just around the corner.

Like most business owners, I had little thought of how the events of September 11, 2001 would impact our company as that day unfolded. Being in the Washington, D.C. area, I was acutely aware of how many people I knew who might've been tragically affected. But overall, the preoccupation was the thought, *What the hell's going on?* It felt as if we'd all been punched in the gut. It felt as if a seismic shift had occurred.

As you know, it took a while before things settled. *Who did this? Would we go to war? If so, with whom? Are we all entering a "new normal"?* It was this last question that had me thinking, sometime the following year, about what would be the new normal in my industry. Our clients, in particular, were significant corporate and government offices. While it was anyone's guess what the post-9/11 world would be like, there was little debate that security issues were never going to be the same.

It's important to continually assess whether you can narrow your focus.

The "high-security sector" had always been there. You had certain buildings and offices that were always among the most comprehensively guarded. I doubt there was ever a time you could just wander the halls of the Justice Department unchecked. But now, it was inevitable that the high-security sector would both change and grow. And we were in an excellent position to address this.

We were certainly not the only company that could meet this coming demand, so I knew I had to act quickly. Training, certifications, systems, protocol… all of that would take time to develop and accomplish, so starting right away was critical. In addition, not just anyone can work within these high-security environments. You probably know the phrase "garbage in, garbage out"—in this case, avoiding it meant establishing unique hiring procedures so that we'd get the right people for the work when the time came.

All in all, it wasn't an overnight thing, as should be expected for such a significant undertaking. I talked with my wife, Danyelle, about needing her help in learning all the details of security clearances, as well as coming on board as our Vice President of Security to help keep us in full compliance. For about two years, we did all the research we could to be sure we'd get this right from the very first client. The last thing we'd want is for word to get around that we bungled our initial high-security gig. And believe me, there was much to go wrong, with all the requirements and protocol. But the effort paid off, and in 2005 we landed our first high-security facility contract.

Let Go of the Good to Make Room for the Great

Since I first heard it, I've liked that saying. It resonates with me. It's a mantra I've always followed because, the reality is, opportunities in business are endless—so it's easy to get sidetracked without focus. Even early on, not long after my parents passed me the business, I recognized we needed to pare down our services. First to go was window washing, and then later we stopped doing snow removal. It's important to continually assess whether you can narrow your focus. And as Mister Kleen celebrated its 30th anniversary in 2006, we took a big step to hone in our core business.

Ernie Sr., Mary Ann, and Cindy Clark at the Mister Kleen 30th anniversary party in 2006.

Though it was fairly new, our high-security facility work was showing tremendous promise. The revenue trajectory we foresaw was incredible, but capitalizing on it would require significant resources. Landing these deals was no small feat, and fulfilling them was even greater. Meanwhile, we had our residential division going strong for 16 years. It was doing well, and the market was growing. It was good—but high-security was great. It was more stable and a better fit for the operation we had built.

So, Dianna and I talked about it. Residential was her baby, and by this time, Dianna had been promoted to General Manager. Since her scope of responsibility was now greater than just the home-cleaning side of our business, she saw the big picture and agreed. We'd let our residential division go. We sold it and honed our services on those needed for commercial, specialty, restoration, and especially high-security jobs.

In hindsight, it was clearly the right move. The return on effort from residential just did not match our long-term strategic goals. It's been my experience as an outside observer of other family businesses that this is one of the things they struggle with most—the 30,000-foot view. It's easy to get stuck in the trenches. I know as well as anyone. But the minute you can pop your head up—or better yet, *make* time to do so—you really need to survey the road ahead. It's often easier to keep doing what you're doing. And this is especially true if it's doing well.

> It's too easy to keep doing what you're doing.

There's that saying, *Don't fix what isn't broken.* Well, sometimes you've got to break it to make it—meaning, make it to the next level. Mister Kleen could still be doing residential. That part of the business wasn't bleeding. It was sustaining itself and contributed reasonably to our bottom line. But if I'd been too far in the weeds, too immersed in the day to day, it's quite likely I would've never seen the high-security sector opportunity. But by taking a strategic look at things and letting go of part of our business, we were able to *double* our annual revenue in the following *seven years*—from $6 million to $12 million. We'd let go of the good to make room for the great. Whether yours is a family business or not, remember to always make time to look down the road. The next big thing, good or bad, may be right in front of you.

Detour Ahead

While we experienced that tremendous growth in the years that followed, it wasn't without setbacks. In fact, a few of those years were the most difficult of my life. I was challenged with several major events in a relatively short period of time:

- Serving BSCAI as an officer and president while the association was going through a major transformation to recover from its downhill trajectory

- My dad's being diagnosed with terminal cancer

- Navigating Mister Kleen through the economic crash of 2007 and 2008

- An audit by the Internal Revenue Service

- And a nearly disastrous contract with a major client

Battle at BSCAI

As of 2006, BSCAI had been in decline for a while and was struggling financially. This was a difficult time for many associations. As such, we set up a turnaround task force, which I participated in significantly as officer of the association. Not knowing the other things that would be hitting me full force in the coming years, I got myself knee deep in the BSCAI situation. One of the first things we did was hire the largest association management firm in the country at the time, Smith Bucklin. It was the best thing we could've done. With them at our side, I joined fellow officers in leading many changes, one of which was a very controversial change that would consume much of the next two years—crafting a co-location deal with ISSA. Now going simply by this name, it had long been known as the International Sanitary Supply Association, and it was the largest manufacturer and supply association in our industry, with more than 6,000 members.

ISSA had long wanted to merge with BSCAI and had even attempted to buy the association. But the prior leadership of BSCAI directed the board to not do it. I saw things differently from my vantage point, being that Mister Kleen's building was not far from BSCAI's headquarters, which allowed me to be more involved between meetings and see what was going on—and more importantly, not going on. To put it simply, the association had been losing significant money over the previous few years, and I didn't see or hear anything that led me to believe this would improve. And so it was that we hired Smith Bucklin and later inked the deal with ISSA. This allowed us to close the longtime BSCAI headquarters in Fairfax, Virginia, and open a new one in Chicago, where both Smith Bucklin and ISSA were located.

The decision seemed quite clear to me—BSCAI's unique ability was fostering networking and education for our industry, and ISSA was putting on the biggest and best trade show in the world for our industry. The mutual benefits were obvious.

Not only that, we had been losing money on our annual trade show and unnecessarily imposing costs on our suppliers, who had to do both the ISSA and BSCAI shows each year. So, we negotiated with ISSA to gain access to their show for our members and eliminated our own show, which of course immediately benefitted our suppliers as well. In addition, we talked ISSA into allowing our members to attend the keynote speakers, which were always big names such as Tony Blair, Donny Deutsch, and David Blaine.

> All challenges are an opportunity to see what people are made of—including those around you.

All in all, the course of events through this time turned out quite positive. And there's no doubt in my mind that BSCAI is a far stronger association as a result. But the entire process pulled away so much of my energy when taking into consideration everything else I had to face. You can only focus on so much at once, and my involvement in the association during this time really stretched my attention thin. However, all challenges are an opportunity to see what people are made of—including those around you. In my case, I am immensely proud of and grateful for the ways Dianna, her son Chad, and our niece

Christy stepped up. They did a great deal of work to help hold down the fort, and Dianna in particular gained a lot of valuable experience and knowledge about the infrastructure of the business—which has made Mister Kleen a more balanced company ever since.

Dad's Diagnosis

Perhaps it was poetic in some way that I was out of town at a BSCAI event, in September of 2007, when I got the news that Dad had been given 12–18 months to live. He had lung cancer that had spread to his brain and liver, and there was nothing they could do. From that point forward, it would be a matter of just making sure his remaining time was as comfortable as possible. Having been through his meningitis diagnosis, when he was basically expected to die, I couldn't help but think, *There must be a way through this, too*. I didn't want to accept the news without a fight.

I wanted to fight it. I wanted *Dad* to fight it. He'd been that scrappy type his whole life—from the time he was a young teen making a living for himself, to being a hard-working father trying to build a bright future for his family, to his improbable though limited recovery from meningitis. He'd made it this far. How could he be beaten now, not even 65 years old yet? Surely, he still had another round in him.

But there was no fight. There was only getting ready for the inevitable. And among all the thoughts that raced through my head, the one that eventually came to the forefront was whether or not Dad's estate was in good order. The truth I had to accept was that he was leaving us; the only question was, is everything how it should be?

Cindy, Dianna, and I met on several occasions to plan for the final day and to determine our next steps. Our family had spent a great deal of time and money a few years prior with our longtime attorney and his associate, with the goal to get things in order now that the family had significant assets. Obviously, we weren't expecting the worst at that point, but we knew it wouldn't be smart to wait any longer. The thing is, after all was said and done, I wasn't completely satisfied that everything was 100 percent right—but I figured we had the basics covered and something was better than nothing.

When the tragic diagnosis later came, I called our attorney to relay the news and ask that he review everything to make sure we were covered. Now, facing Dad's terminal prognosis, it was imperative things were in order. So the attorney looked over the work he'd done and called me back. "Um," he said, "we have a few changes to make." Remember what I wrote earlier about trusting your gut? Well, mine was starting to send me signals. We met with the attorney a few times, which ended up amounting to a lot of wheel-spinning, and I realized we needed a Plan B. He'd made some mistakes, and I wasn't comfortable these were going to be corrected as we needed.

I started interviewing estate attorneys and found one who came highly regarded and I liked. I paid him to review the trust, and he very calmly and reassuringly told me we had some changes to make. It was terrible timing—Dad was being treated for cancer, and I had to drag him and Mom into meetings with this new attorney. (Steve Nadler was there with us, too, as a witness and trusted consultant.) But we had to make these updates to attempt to preserve the assets for which my parents had worked so hard. After we got it all ironed out, I asked the attorney what would've happened if I'd not had this reviewed and redone—he said we would've lost *several hundreds of thousands of dollars* to estate taxes. Like I said, trust your gut.

Through the course of the next year, Dad's health declined as expected. Eventually, he was attended to at home by a hospice organization called Capital Caring, which took phenomenal care of him. People who do that work are to be commended. They made my father's final months as best as could be, and they were tremendously supportive for all of us in the family. I don't know how we would've done it without them. Eventually, the day had to come. And so it was, with the love of so many people surrounding him, Ernest Clark Sr. finally passed away on February 20, 2009, at the age of 66.

The IRS Pays a Visit and the Economy Take a Dive

Sometimes life has a way of coming at you from every direction all at once. It couldn't be enough that I had to work through the many emotional and practical issues of my dad's final months. Apparently, it was my time to take on much more.

In the thick of everything in 2008, Mister Kleen was hit with an Internal Revenue Service audit. We hadn't done anything wrong; some IRS audits are triggered automatically and some are triggered randomly. You aren't always told why your account was flagged, but the results are pretty much the same—it's nothing you want to go through. I'm happy to report that we came out fine, with no adjustments or penalties. I knew our accounting was solid, so I wasn't really worried, but it was an absolutely laborious process for a company our size. I think I would've rather carried a sack of bricks on my back the whole time.

Almost precisely corresponding to the months between my dad's diagnosis and his passing, from 2007 through 2008 and into 2009, the economy went into an infamous free fall that threatened to match the Great Depression. Unless you were living in a cave at the time, you know that unemployment skyrocketed, banks collapsed, the stock market bottomed out, the housing market tanked, and people lost their retirement funds. While I'm grateful we weren't among the many businesses that failed during this time, we had to make numerous course corrections and keep everything closely watched. The commercial real estate market hit us hard, when facilities management companies tightened up their finances and left us in a precarious situation. It was a saving grace that we'd focused in the high-security sector because matters surrounding security are often the last to be affected financially; a high-security facility isn't going to suddenly contract a cut-rate cleaning firm with minimal credentials to save money. However, we did have to make some cost concessions and certainly felt the impact. Though we were able to ultimately weather the economic storm, it was compounded by a perhaps greater threat—an incredibly consuming contract that was practically set up to fail.

Let Go of the Bad to Make Room for the Better

As you recall from Chapter 9, we landed a major deal one time that I was very hesitant about. Well, this is the one of which I was speaking. I'm not sure this contract would've been good at any time, but it was particularly exhausting for us as a company, and especially me, with everything else going on. It sucked away valuable resources and required a huge investment on our part. There's an old Chinese proverb, *He who chases many rabbits catches none.* That is about where things were for us as a company and me as its leader. The focus we had in 2006 was now diminished—but we were at the point where the only way past it was through it. It was head down, plow forward. As you know, we ultimately were dropped from the contract at its renewal two years later. What you don't know is that this amounted to nearly 30 percent of our revenues at the time. Clearly, this was a huge loss. Or was it?

I wrote earlier about letting go of the good to make room for the great. In this case, there was no good, really, to be found. So, sometimes, you have to let go of the bad to make room for the better. There's a business concept that's cropped up over the past decade or so, that was initially seen as radical but has taken root among some CEOs and entrepreneurs—fire your worst customers or clients. The idea is that you should regularly review and grade your clients, based on how good a fit they are for your business. This might be based on factors such as how quickly they pay or their contribution to your bottom line, but mostly it comes down to whether it's a *healthy, positive, and mutually beneficial relationship*. That's what we all seek in life, right? Well, business is no different. So with this criteria, grade your clients. If they earn a "D" or "F," fulfill your existing agreement, collect what they owe you, and let them go. If they earn a "C" or "B," see if there's a way to improve their grade in whatever ways they're falling short. And of course, if they earn an "A," do everything you can to maintain the relationship and devote your resources to finding other "A" clients. Often, your "A" clients are your best resource for finding other "A" clients—birds of a feather flock together—and they're the most likely to invest in other services or products your business offers.

So while we weren't the ones letting go of this contract, which was clearly an "F," I know now that's what we should've done. But because it accounted for nearly a third of our revenues, and during an economically rocky time, quite frankly I don't know that I would've been bold enough to fire this client. Thus, this was truly a blessing in disguise; we were forced to let go of the bad to make room for the better. Undoubtedly, all the time, energy, and resources we would've had to continue to pour into that contract, had it been renewed, we were able to instead put toward better business relationships.

CHAPTER 12

GETTING OUT OF THE WEEDS

WHEN LIFE PUTS YOU THROUGH THE WRINGER LIKE IT did to me from 2007 through 2010, you can't help but come out of it a changed person. Of course, on a higher level, this is why these things happen. We're all meant to continue growing in our lives, but we tend to be reluctant since "growing" almost always equates to "pain." Have you ever personally grown much during the sunny times of your life? Probably not. Most people don't. So, it's only with the perspective that we'll come out of the rough times a better person that we can accept the challenges life throws our way.

I could probably write a book just on what I learned from this time frame. So, let's just say that it all came down to realizing that I had simply created a job for myself at Mister Kleen—a nice one in most ways, and certainly well paying, but a job nonetheless. As a CEO, you're either working *on* the business or working *in* it. Small distinction in language, but a big distinction in meaning. And I'd come to learn that I was most certainly working *in* my business.

Remember what I wrote earlier about maintaining a strategic perspective, and how it enabled me to see the high-security sector opportunity we moved into? Well, I'd fallen back down into the weeds. Sure, some of it was due to things I couldn't have foreseen, but I'd still played a part in landing back in that position. Heck, I think I was past the weeds and into a swamp.

The clarity that was life's two-by-four hitting me upside the head was that I needed a way out of being too involved in the day-to-day business—but I wasn't seeing exactly how I could change that. Sometimes you get swallowed by what you're doing because that's all you've been doing. We tend to see things as they are, not as they could be. I remember one time learning about early aircraft designs, why the cockpit was on the top. For many years, cockpits stayed on the top of planes because that's simply how it had been. It never occurred to anyone to put the cockpit *inside* the plane, though aerodynamically this made more sense. Finally, though, someone had this idea, the technology was created to make it possible, and the commercial jets of today are designed this way. I don't know if this history is true or myth, but I was definitely still "seeing the cockpit on top of the plane."

> CEOs and entrepreneurs thrive on challenges, and being too immersed in the business feels stagnant.

The other potential hindrance when you're bogged down in the business is that things can start to look bland for the future, both for yourself and the company. Perhaps it's because your creative energies are zapped by the mundane and your ability to *envision* the future is compromised. CEOs and entrepreneurs thrive on challenges, and being too immersed in the business feels stagnant. All of this was certainly true for me.

Interestingly, for some years at this point, I'd been considering joining an organization called Strategic Coach, started and run by Dan Sullivan and Babs Smith back in the 1980s. It had grown to be a premier educational and networking organization for high-level entrepreneurs and business owners from all over the world. I attended one of their all-day seminars in 2006, but with all the events in the years to come, I'd put off joining. I wanted to make the commitment of time and money when I could be fully present and able to make use of it.

Well, suddenly and not surprisingly, Strategic Coach seemed very attractive to me come 2011. Things had settled, and I could throw myself into what the group had to offer. It was time to make it happen. And man, am I glad I did. The funny thing is, I have to admit, when people ask me exactly how it's helped, it can be hard to put into words. Part of it is being around people who've likely shared what you're facing or near enough that they can understand it. One reason for this is that Coach, as we call it, is segregated into levels based on the income of your business. This may sound elitist, but it's actually very practical—the challenges facing the owner of a five-person business grossing $900,000 per year can be quite different than those facing the owner of a much larger company. So again, you're set in the organization to interact with people close to your level of business. Another reason behind the like-mindedness is the commitment required to join and participate. There is a financial commitment, in membership and travel costs, and a time commitment, in quarterly meetings and travel. Though Coach is based in the United States and Canada, its members come from every continent. My going to Toronto from Washington, D.C. every 90 days is not that big a deal, but it certainly would be for someone coming from Asia or Australia. So, simply put, Coach members are serious and dedicated.

The other major benefit, the flipside to the time and travel commitment, is that you have time to focus. Dan Sullivan and his team instill in you the importance of dedicating your time while you're there—no babysitting your iPhone and email, no taking calls, no laptops in the room. Everything we do is on paper, written with a good old-fashioned pencil. The delete key is that little red rubber eraser. In our omni-digital world of today, this all may sound like kindergarten without the crayons and white paste. But let me tell you, this is precisely what so many business people at this level need—time disconnected from their devices, time away from demands, time to focus. We're given permission to say we're not available, something many CEOs and entrepreneurs ironically have a hard time giving themselves. The value of having this quality time, although only once a quarter, is immense. I hear again and again from other members how much it means to them. And of course, the Coach program teaches you to build this much-needed time into your schedule on your own. It's called *Strategic*

Coach because the goal is to learn to operate your business and life from a strategic level.

Circling back to Mister Kleen, if I had to pick the one thing that has come out of my time with Coach, it would be the hiring of our Chief Operating Officer. The program helped me to see that if I didn't bring on someone to help run the day-to-day business of Mister Kleen, I'd be forever vulnerable to another trip into the swamp. Furthermore, down the road, I could never turn over the business to someone if it were 100 percent dependent on my expertise and participation. Again, that's working *in* a business, not *on* it. So, in February 2012, I hired our first COO. These couple of years with her onboard, they've been like no other in my time running Mister Kleen. I can truly ask myself, *Why didn't I do this sooner?* But then again, things happen when they do for a reason, and perhaps the reason was her being available. If that's why I unknowingly waited, then it was worth the wait. With her help running the day-to-day operations, I've been able to identify and execute my top three functions as President and CEO:

1. Provide the vision and strategy
2. Recruit the best talent and support them
3. Monitor the gauges I've put in place to ensure a highly efficient organization

I can finally say I'm out of the weeds. And it's no coincidence that, since those incredibly challenging years between 2007 and 2010, Mister Kleen has grown at a pace far beyond what it had during any other time. We now service millions of square feet of commercial office and high-security space in over 75 locations, through the work of more than 400 employees.

And in 2012, we grossed more revenue than in our first 20 years combined—surpassing the eight-figure dollar level for the third year in a row.

Finish what you start. As you know, I believe this firmly, and though I haven't literally finished my time at Mister Kleen, there's a sense of closure in some ways. Having in place Dianna, Christy, Chad, and of course a COO, as well as my other management team, I now have the freedom to put my mind to the strategic aspects and broader goals of the business—as well as focus on my unique abilities and how they can best serve the company's mission. Having taken things to this higher level gives me a strong sense of having finished what I started when Mom and Dad passed the torch to me. That means a lot. I feel I've done them proud, and I hope so of everyone else in my family. It's been difficult at times to bring these two ideals together, but I truly feel we've built a family-owned business *and* professionally managed company.

SAY 'PLEASE' AND 'THANK YOU'

Three generations of Clarks in the family business, shown in 2007, left to right: Mary Ann, Ernie Sr., Christy, Chad, Dianna, and Ernie Jr.

CHAPTER 13

FAMILY BUSINESS MATTERS

Instilling Respect and Appreciation

Work Hard, Show Up on Time, Do What You Say, and *Finish What You Start.* They're not just the titles of the first four sections of this book, they're guiding principles for my life and my business—as I believe they should be for any life and business.

Say "Please" and "Thank You" seems like it should be the natural follow-up to the guiding principles of the previous four—and it is that. But it has a broader meaning as well. It is also about instilling respect and appreciation in the succeeding generations that will benefit from all your hard work, your showing up, your doing what you say, your finishing what you start.

As I mentioned in the introduction, there is an old adage— "rags to riches to rags in three generations"—that exists among many languages and societies. In China, for example, they say "rice paddy to rice paddy." Regardless of the culture, the maxim warns, *You can't sustain wealth through three generations.* The first generation builds the wealth with hard work, discipline, and sacrifice. The second generation, their children, witnesses the hard work and sacrifice of their parents, stewards that wealth, and builds upon it. The third generation, knowing only the fruits of their ancestors' hard work, and the ease that came with it, squanders that wealth, bringing *that* generation and their descendents back down to the rags part of the story.

It's important to note here that I'm not necessarily talking about financial wealth. The saying and its application extend through all types of "wealth," meaning abundance, which can include friends, achievements, fame, creations, and even spiritual support. Financial wealth, by itself, would be quite empty.

So, I'm doing my absolute best to ensure we avoid that path right now. How do you raise a child that has only known ease and prosperity, to appreciate hard work, showing up on time, doing what they say, finishing what they start, and saying "please" and "thank you"? More perplexing, how do you build a business and set of financial resources that will endure past the third generation and survive?

Three Generations—One Set of Rules

A third generation of Clarks is already in place at Mister Kleen, though not yet at the helm. Cindy's daughter, Christy, is Director of Field Services; Dianna's son, Chad, is Director of Sales and Marketing. They are exemplary managers and very good at what they do. And like all the Clarks, they first experienced going on jobs when they were just kids helping out.

Christy has been with Mister Kleen for 17 years now, having held a number of different positions, and is superb at her job. She worked with us for a short time as an administrative assistant just out of high school before Dianna and I encouraged her to broaden her work experience through other jobs. A few years later, she came back to Mister Kleen with an enhanced perspective and climbed her way from the bottom up to her current position.

Chad's story unfolded much the same way, having joined our Specialty Services Division straight out of high school. Because of this division's unset schedule—being called in the middle of the night, holidays, and weekends for flood and fire clean-up—the hours were hard to embrace. Between this and his lack of work experience elsewhere, Dianna and I did the same as we'd done with Christy, giving him a nudge out of the nest. Chad got a job as a Domino's Pizza driver and, over a couple years, worked his way up to store manager. One Christmas, I asked him how it was going, and he replied, "It's fine, but I work six days a week, 12 hours a day." How ironic!

So, we spoke to him about rejoining Mister Kleen—and as of the writing of this book, he's about to celebrate 12 years with us.

*I believe it's important to have family members **first** work elsewhere for at least a couple of years before joining the family business. This enables them to get exposed to the rules and responsibilities of business in general, before joining the family business.*

A lot of clients and vendors will remark to me about Christy's and Chad's professionalism, knowledge, competence, and courtesy, to which I always joke, "The beatings really paid off." Okay, there was none of that. But neither was there any gold-plated path or nepotism. When Chad rejoined Mister Kleen, he started out scrubbing floors; Christy started in lower-level administrative positions. They both served in those roles for more than a year before moving up, but only a notch—Chad to floor-scrubbing supervisor and Christy to helping and overseeing residential crews. They were then moved to sales, marketing, and operations. These paths are no different than they would be for any other employee in the same situation, because I do my best to ensure there is only one set of rules at Mister Kleen that apply to family and

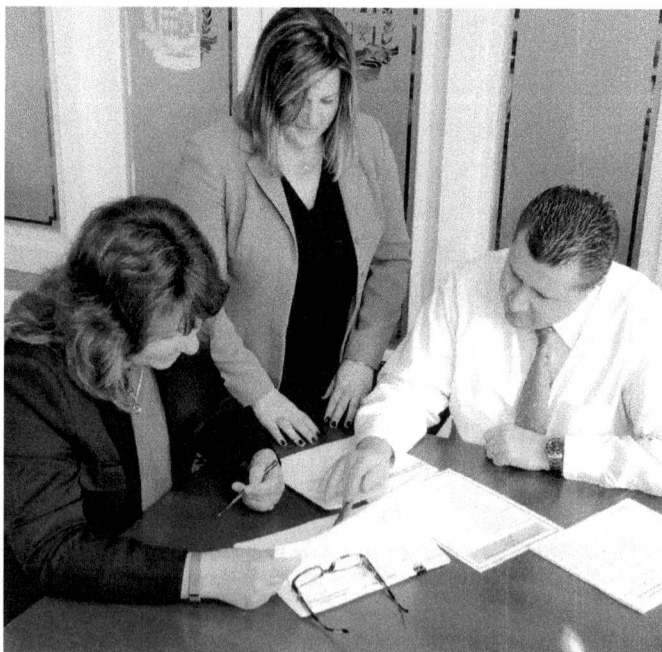

Dianna, Christy, and Chad review company reports and projections.

non-family members alike.

Likewise, I have an employee directive that applies to everyone: *Train, train and re-train*. Because Christy and Chad were looking to be with Mister Kleen in the long term, to make a career of it, I had to add to that directive another element: *Cross-train*. I firmly

> I firmly believe you must know how to do everything you're going to manage.

believe you must know how to do everything you're going to manage—and after having spent a year or more in the trenches, and in every department at the company, Christy and Chad most certainly do.

Bring in the Professionals

There's a special challenge in running a family business, one that doesn't exist in any other operation—and not all business owners have the necessary skills to do it well. Managing your children, or your sister's or brother's children, can be a particularly tricky and precarious proposition. You either manage them well in the business, and then probably have a strained relationship at home or on holidays, or you don't manage them well, and that's not good for the business or the kid. However, there is another option, which is what I did—bring in someone with an outside perspective to mentor them and provide space between your family relationship and your boss/employee relationship. This may be someone literally working within the business, as I'll discuss more in a moment, or it may be through coaching and training. With Christy and Chad, I provided them access to professional business coaching, sent them to Dale Carnegie programs and other external specialized training, and ensured they received industry certification as Registered Building Service Managers. Having done all this and seen the positive results, I truly believe it's best for family members in your business to grow under the leadership and direction of people who aren't family.

Bringing in professional help also makes possible one of the tenets of Dan Sullivan's Strategic Coach program—focus on your unique ability. Sullivan encourages business owners to concentrate on the things they do best and that give them the most energy, and to delegate the rest. I'd spent years working every facet of Mister Kleen: paying vendors, sales and marketing, human resources, legal, accounting, the all-consuming operations, and of course, opening and sorting the mail. It was time to step back, get out of the weeds, and focus only on the areas I enjoyed most.

As I mentioned earlier, the single most important thing so far to come from my time in Strategic Coach was the hiring of our Chief Operating Officer. Our COO performs many jobs, but a crucial one is to provide a buffer between my role as brother and uncle, and my role as President and CEO. This helps us keep work life at work, and home life at home. Our policy of not having family report to family has allowed us to keep things professional when they need to be, and family at other times.

Of course, our COO is also on board to help our business reach the next level. A lot of family members—and hundreds of non-family members—rely on Mister Kleen for their livelihood. I can't just arrive at a certain point and say, "Well, I'm happy." I have to allow people to have a good quality of life, a respectable income level, and growth in their careers. Bringing on our COO, and stepping back from daily operating details, has permitted me to focus on this goal as well.

Walking Your Talk

If instilling respect and appreciation in succeeding generations is part of my "Say 'Please' and 'Thank You'" mission, then I have to walk my talk.

I am exceedingly grateful and unimaginably appreciative of all that has transpired to bring my family and me to where we are today. And I know the long and hard road it took to get us here. There's a myth in the law-of-the-jungle, survival-of-the-fittest paradigm that is supposed to govern our lives. The reality is, numerous people helped me out along my path.

Because so many people in so many ways helped us to make Mister Kleen what it is today, I make sure the company gives back and supports organizations that make a difference. In addition to her professional duties, Dianna has been a tremendous leader in our community involvement—she, Christy, and Chad participate actively in supporting many causes. I'm proud of their passion for this aspect of our business.

Some of the organizations we have supported over the years include The American Cancer Society, Inova Alexandria Hospital Foundation, Five Talents X-Out Poverty, Whitman Walker Clinic, the Joan Hisaoka "Make a Difference" Gala, Adopt A Family, and the Avon Walk for Breast Cancer.

Saying "please" and "thank you" can be more than just

words. Backing up your gratitude with action can be a great way to demonstrate the respect and appreciation you feel for all that's come your way.

CHAPTER 14

SUCCESSION

The Merit of Performance

In Thomas J. Stanley's book *The Millionaire Next Door*, Stanley talks about self-made millionaires who succeed in tough, hands-on industries like ours. Even though they know how to achieve success, they don't want their children to endure what they went through. I think this is a mistake.

A good friend and financial advisor whose clients include many high net worth and high income individuals has said to me, "You know how many family businesses I see where the kids are worthless?"

Worthless. It's a harsh word. But as he's watched arrogant, self-absorbed, entitled children squander the resources their parents worked so long and hard to create, he can't help but shudder.

My wife, Danyelle, and I have one daughter, Lexi, who just started high school. So in terms of age, she is a full generation behind Christy and over half a generation behind Chad—although, in the family tree, all three are part of the third generation.

Lexi will be driving next year, and she's eyeing a new car with some flash and cachet; she also enjoys all the clothes and gadgets so relentlessly marketed to her generation. Even though giving her some of these things wouldn't break the bank, my wife and I deliberately tell her "no." We do so because life will tell her, "no." She needs to understand that.

Lexi plays two sports, is required to get good grades, and we demand she exhibit respect, kindness, and courtesy to everyone she meets, especially her elders. At the end of the day, regardless of the fate of Mister Kleen, if anyone were to ever describe her as spoiled, Danyelle and I would consider that a parental failure.

We're not sure what path Lexi will choose in her adult life; at this point, she's talking equine veterinarian or possibly sports medicine, but those choices are expected to change, as well they should at her age. Lexi will go to college. She will be the first in our family to go to college full time, and we're aiming for a great school. But one thing I do know for sure: If our daughter decides she *does* want to join Mister Kleen in the future, she'll have to go off and work elsewhere for a couple of years before joining the family business. She'll have to earn her keep based on the merit of her performance, not her family connections.

Right Here and Right Now

And so, I'm feeling cautiously optimistic. Both my niece and nephew, and my daughter, consistently say "please" and "thank you." And there's a great deal of time and care being put into succession planning, so I'm betting Mister Kleen will continue to defy the odds, and our business and resources will survive the third generation. What my parents, my sisters, and I worked so hard to build will not go back to rags.

As for me, I have no plans of going anywhere anytime soon. I love the hunt; I love putting things together; I love watching them grow. I keep my eye on our business's vision, my pulse on all the gauges and indicators that I've put into place, and my nose in all that's current and cutting-edge in our industry.

But, then again, you never do know. As with my father, life happens. And sometimes it happens without warning when you're not even looking. So having a good plan in place for all contingencies, in life and work, is imperative.

Looking back, I sometimes can't believe how things turned out. If I blink, I can go back to those days of vacuuming up sewer slime in the dead of night or shoveling blocks and blocks of snow in 20-degree cold. I have to laugh. I never could have imagined my life as it is today. My parents, sisters, and I have created a family that celebrates together and works together, something less and less common in this day and age.

My mother Mary Ann, my sister Cindy, my sister Dianna, my niece Christy, my nephew Chad, my daughter Lexi, and my wife Danyelle have all gone on this journey with me, many of them right from the start. Together, they have helped not only make me a successful man, but a happy and fulfilled one.

It is my deepest hope that my father, looking down on us, is proud of all he sees. And whether or not there is a divine hereafter that scoops us up when this is all said and done, I am so grateful and proud, right here and right now, to be a part of all of you.

ACKNOWLEDGEMENTS

The writing and creation of a book is a team effort, both during the process and in all the years leading up to it. Many people have made this book possible in one way or another, and I'm truly grateful to you:

My late father, Ernest Clark Sr., for laying such a solid foundation for all of us and for teaching us things we would have never learned in college.

My mother, Mary Ann Clark, for her unwavering love of family and for always setting such a fine example for all of us... and I especially appreciate your help with this book.

My loving and supportive wife, Danyelle... my true soul mate who has always believed in me, even when I was a window washer!

Our entire family for always being so united and cohesive. Mister Kleen would not be what it is today without each and every one of you helping in some way. A special thank-you to my sister Dianna for her hard work, dedication, and for always being there.

My amazing daughter, Lexi, for giving me so much to be proud of.

The entire Mister Kleen Team... thank you for all that you do and for allowing me the time and freedom from the day-to-day to write this book.

Our clients for believing in us and giving us an opportunity.

We appreciate you and hope you enjoy learning more about Mister Kleen "from behind the curtain!"

My friend and accountant Steve Nadler for being by our side from the beginning.

Howard Cohen of Daycon for listening to me in that board meeting more than 20 years ago and later spending several late nights working with our team… you've been a good friend and service partner.

Kim Lysik DiSanti of Total Strategy for her coaching, counseling, and friendship to our family for more than 10 years. A special thanks for your help with this book.

Dan Sullivan and the rest of the Strategic Coach team for giving me the confidence, clarity, and tools needed to get this book started.

My Peer Group, Vistage, ELK Group, and all the other business groups I've participated in over the years. These forums and people have been instrumental in teaching me what to do and sometimes what *not* to do.

To the BSCAI Turnaround Task Force, Founders Circle donors, and fellow officers of BSCAI who volunteered and donated selflessly for an organization we all believe in. A special thank-you to the folks at Smith Bucklin for being there for us at the right time. I know it wasn't easy for any of us, and we should all be proud of the transformation we led BSCAI through.

Mona Kuljurgis and Andrew Chapman for all your help and patience with getting this book accomplished.

The Clarks, from left to right: Mary Ann, Ernie Jr., Dianna, and Ernie Sr.

ABOUT THE AUTHOR

Ernie Clark Jr., CBSE, is the president of Mister Kleen Maintenance Co., a leading provider of contract cleaning services to commercial and high-security facilities in the Washington, D.C., area. He has been active in the family business since his parents started it in 1976, working from the entry level up to his current position.

An industry leader in establishing best practices, Clark is actively involved in many business groups and has been the recipient of numerous community-service and industry awards. He holds the highest professional designation in his field, Certified Building Service Executive, and is past president of both Building Service Contractors Association International and Capital Association of Building Service Contractors.

Clark lives in Northern Virginia with his wife of more than two decades, Danyelle, and their daughter Lexi.

ORDER THIS BOOK

This book is exclusively available on Amazon.com. For bulk purchases, special orders, or author inquiries, please email:

Book@MisterKleen.com

Remember, for every copy purchased through Amazon.com, all proceeds go to the Cancer Research Institute. See the first page of this book for more details.